Themes, Dreams, and Weems

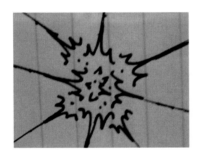

Bill Ectric

Themes, Dreams, and Weems

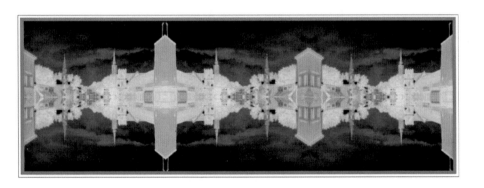

Bill Ectric

Astral Pages

Themes, Dreams, and Weems

Copyright 2019 by Bill Ectric

ISBN: 9781074243302

Astral Pages

While drinking tea,

I REMEMBER

A Highly Magnified History and dark clouds of celestial dust that change according to news, DREAMS also affecting lifestyle in a few of the acts that played there: BARKING paperback books, and *Artisans.*

$1 50

August Strindberg's Inferno
This article first appeared on Literary Kicks, June 2, 2011

Alchemy, schizophrenia, witchcraft, and religious fanaticism, all leavened with a knowing wink of humor, *Inferno*, by Swedish author August Strindberg is an early example of the "unreliable narrator" literary device, in which the reader learns that the storyteller is seeing things from a distorted perspective. It is also deliciously macabre, if you like that sort of thing.

The Inferno is far from Strindberg's most famous work. In 1879, he became famous in Northern Europe with the publication of what is often described as the first modern Swedish novel, *The Red Room*. Set in Stockholm, *The Red Room* is a satire dealing with compromise and corruption in politics, journalism, and business in general. Strindberg wrote over 60 plays and is probably best known for his 1888 play *Miss Julie*, which told a tale of power and sex within high and low social classes. Other plays include *The Father, Creditors,* and *The Ghost Sonata*. He was also an essayist, a painter (two of his friends were Edvard Munch and Paul Gauguin), and based on at least one photograph, a guitarist.

Strindberg's early plays were in the naturalist style, closely associated with realism, but that all changed when he got out of the hospital after a so-called nervous breakdown. Many of his later works are now considered precursors to surrealism and expressionism. *The Ghost Sonata* features ghosts, a woman who becomes a mummy, and cook who sucks all the nourishment out of the food before serving it.

Not surprisingly for someone influenced in varying degrees by Charles Darwin, Friedrich Nietzsche, Edgar Allen Poe, and William Shakespeare, Strindberg often found himself at odds with both Church and State. The State tried to censor his plays for sexual content and for criticism of the government. The Church accused him of blasphemy for mocking the Holy Communion in his 1884 book *Getting Married*. Critics found fault with his work even as his popularity grew with the public. Financial problems led to bankruptcy. It has been speculated that these adversities, along with stress from this second divorce and estrangement from his children (his third divorce would come later), compounded by the use of alcohol and absinthe, culminated in the psychotic episode that landed him in the hospital while he was travelling abroad in France.

There is some disagreement as to how much of *The Inferno* is based on an actual nervous breakdown and how much Strindberg embellished and exaggerated his madness to make a better story. Having just finished reading *Inferno*, I have to believe that, if Strindberg really went temporarily insane in the mid-1890s, he certainly recovered enough to write a candidly self-aware book about the experience.

This book may make you think of Philip K. Dick's pseudo-religious experience involving a pink light sending information into his brain, or Jack Kerouac's crack-up in *Big Sur*. But what makes *The Inferno* so fun is Strindberg's enthusiastic sense of self-parody. Hunter S. Thompson once said, "buy the ticket, take the ride," and in this book Strindberg takes us right along beside him. It may also remind you of Salvador Dali's self-described paranoiac-critical method, in which the artist sees through the eyes of a madman but paints what he sees with the lucid skill of a draftsman.

The main character of *Inferno*, presumably Strindberg himself, wanders

4

from place to place in search of peace of mind, experiencing bouts of paranoia, hallucinations, apophenia (imagining profound connections in random coincidences), and pareidolia (seeing faces and other shapes in ordinary objects, like when someone claims to see the face of Jesus in a piece of toast). In fact, Strindberg did dabble in alchemy and religious mysticism. Here is a typical passage from *Inferno*:

> In my fireplace I burn coals which, because of their round and regular shape, are called "monks' heads." One day when the fire is nearly extinguished, I take out a mass of coal of fantastic shape. It resembles a cock's head with a splendid comb joined to what looks like a human trunk with twisted limbs. It might have been a demon from some mediaeval witches' Sabbath.
>
> The second day I take out again a fine group of two gnomes or drunken dwarfs, who embrace each other while their clothes flutter in the wind. It is a masterpiece of primitive culture.
>
> The third day it is a Madonna and Child in the Byzantine style, of incomparable beauty of outline. After I have drawn copies of all three in black chalk, I place them on my table. A friendly painter visits me; he regards the three statuettes with growing *curiosity and asks who has" made" them. In order to try him, I mention the name of a Norwegian sculptor." No," he says," I should rather be inclined to ascribe them to Kittelsen the famous illustrator of the Swedish legends."*

This made me smile, because most of Strindberg's original readers would have recognized the reference to Theodor Kittelsen, an illustrator known for his depictions of trolls, ogres, and spirits for books of Norwegian folk and fairy tales. The modern equivalent to the above exchange might be someone building a sculpture out of cereal boxes and attributing it to Rodin, only to have a skeptical art critic look at it and say, "More like Warhol, if you ask me."

Strindberg recovered from his breakdown and continued to write more successfully than ever, garnering acclaim and awards for his work.

German theater and film director Max Reinhardt staged some of Strindberg's plays in Germany. Reinhardt and Strindberg were key figures in the creation of the chamber play, which can be performed with a small cast, in a small space, with a minimum of sets and costumes.

Strindberg spent the last four years of his life in a building he called The Blue Tower in Stockholm, Sweden. This building is now The Strindberg Museum, containing a library of some 4,000 works by or about Strindberg, as well as exhibitions on various aspects of his career.

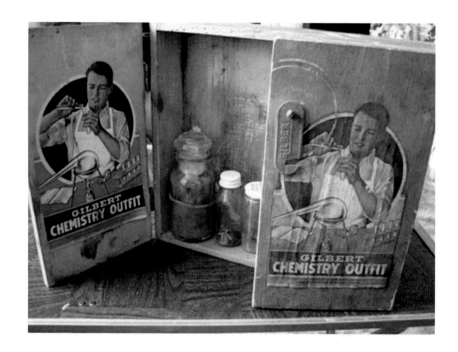

He halts, and searches with his eye

By far the strangest, and most thrilling,

teachers have found

structure and quantum

theory root. April is the month in which old plants should be divided, and rooted branches removed from the parent plant.

WHAT AM I SUPPOSED TO...

make jewelry with?

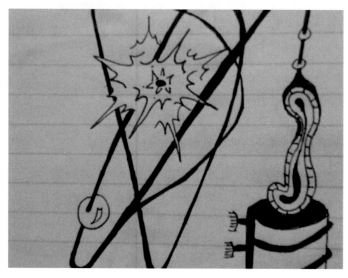

Parson Weems' Tales:
Biography, Historical Fiction, or Fake News?

Mason Locke Weems (1759 – 1825) was a writer, book store owner, book agent, and an Episcopalian minister (or parson). Born in Maryland, he and his family lived in Dumfries, Virginia when he began travelling extensively to preach and sell books. He is most famous for writing the first biography of George Washington, *The Life of Washington* (1800). It was Parson Weems who wrote the story about a youthful George Washington chopping down a cherry tree – a story that everyone now delights in pronouncing a myth and a fiction. But what if the story is true?

"The evidence that the story is true is equal to the evidence that it is false," says Philip Levy in an online interview (Mount Vernon.org).

Dr. Emorest Fogloft theorizes that, under certain unusual conditions, the act of writing a story causes it to happen retroactively. He believes that Parson Weems may have tapped into an energy that created those conditions. Fogloft also suggests that Montague Summers and Michael Sadleir somehow generated the "horrid mystery" novels listed in Jane Austin's Gothic novel, *Northanger Abbey* (1818), even though the novels were all published before Summers and Sadleir were born. The protagonist of *Northanger Abbey*, a fan of mystery and horror fiction, is given seven Gothic novels, which Austin names by title and author. Most readers and scholars assumed that the seven titles listed were not real books. Montague Summers and Michael Sadlier researched the matter and discovered that the books existed.

Fogloft dismisses all scientific evidence that indicates writing a book can make the book appear years earlier. He argues that, "Most critics of my work are too quick to bring up the impossibility of time travel. Quantum physics suggests that time travel requires passing through a cosmic "tunnel" known as a wormhole. Wormholes would collapse almost as soon as they form, allowing only tiny particles to pass through them. The law of relativity suggests you must reach the speed of light to travel in time. I know these things. But these hindrances do not apply to my theory. For one thing, the raw materials are already in the past. By raw materials I mean paper and ink and printing presses. They need not travel through a wormhole at all. Only words, or the image of words – and remember, image is light – or even the mental energy of thinking, the microscopic synapses in the brain...but this is neither the time nor the place to elaborate. *Time-resolved crystallography* may be involved."

We can be sure that Levy was not endorsing Professor Fogloft's theory when he wrote, coincidentally, that "George Allan England was half right when he claimed that time and retelling had made it so the Cherry Tree "crystallized" into fact. It might not be fact, but its retellings and their effect on the landscape had crystallized the old tree into history."

Works Cited

Levy, Philip. *Where the Cherry Tree Grew*. St. Martin's Press. Kindle Edition.

Mount Vernon.org. "Where the Cherry Tree Grew: An Interview with Phillip Levy." Mount Vernon.org. https://www.mountvernon.org/george-washington/facts/where-the-cherry-tree-grew-an-interview-with-phillip-levy/. Accessed 19 June 2019.

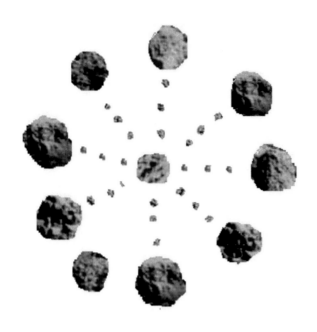

Excerpt from Professor Fogloft's Dissertation:

Transcending Time and Space in Silko's *Ceremony*

In 1880, the United States government told John Elk, a Winnebago Indian, that he could not vote, even though he was born in the United States. The law said Indians were not citizens. The same year, a British mathematician named Charles Hinton wrote an article explaining why time is the fourth dimension. John Elk took his case all the way to the supreme court, which ruled against him in 1884, the same year Edwin A. Abbott, another Englishman, published his whimsical primer on relativity called *Flatland: A Romance of Many Dimensions*. These seemingly unrelated concurrences may not rise to a mystical level of synchronicity, but they do illustrate a fascinating enigma. How can the power of words, *the letter of the law*, project a man into an alternate reality, a parallel dimension if you will, where he is a foreigner in the land of his birth and continued residence? Momaday writes, "Words are intrinsically powerful. They are magical. By means of words can one bring about physical change in the universe" (15,16). This paper will examine how words, when employed ceremonially, can transcend time and space to achieve either magic or witchery, primarily focusing on *Ceremony*, a novel by Leslie Marmon Silko.

Also in 1884, U.S. President Chester A. Arthur initiated the International Meridian Conference in Washington, D.C., where twenty-six nations met to standardize, or *lock down*, time schedules for ships, railroads, and other forms of commerce and transportation. Time, a phenomenon once perceived in the natural movement of celestial bodies and biological rhythms, became a taskmaster driving international commerce. Ironically, while scientists, mathematicians, and politician in both Great Britain and the United States made great strides toward comprehending and harnessing the invisible fabric of time and space, their countries of origin still maintained archaic imperialistic holds in Egypt, Africa, India, and entire nations of native-born Americans.

The American Indians who greeted the first European settlers had no need for standardized time and rigid schedules. Allen writes, "The achronological [non-chronological] time sense of tribal people results from tribal beliefs about the nature of reality, beliefs based on ceremonial understandings rather than on industrial, theological, or agricultural orderings" (149) and "Achronology is the favored structuring device of American Indian novelists since N. Scott Momaday selected it for organizing *House Made of Dawn*" (147). Silko's novel, *Ceremony*, certainly fits into the category of non-chronological narrative. The story moves from Tayo's stay in the V.A. hospital upon returning from war, to his childhood, to his experiences during the war, to drinking with his fellow veteran's after his release from the V.A. hospital, to young adulthood, and so on.

Silko begins *Ceremony* with a montage of sights and sounds, using that most conducive to all fragmented-time backdrops: the dream. The protagonist, Tayo, who is half Pueblo Indian and half white, suffers from PTSD after returning from World War II. His symptoms include depression, physical illness upon eating, insomnia, and, when he does manage to fall asleep, nightmares. The dream sequence works well to initiate the reader into the nonchronological narrative structure because everyone understands the disconnected nature of dreams. The sights and sounds of his dream basically summarize the novel's disparate slices of time and space, letting them flow freely and rotate to the surface at random like findings from a Magic 8 Ball fortune teller. Tayo hears a man singing in Spanish; Japanese voices, angry and loud; Laguna Indian voices of his relatives; strange women's voices; loud music from a garish juke box. He sees the garish light from the juke box, the colts that he and his uncle had taken to the mountains, colored threads from Grandmas sewing basket, Japanese soldiers, the skin of corpses, and the face of a Japanese soldier changing into the face of his Uncle Joisah. Having read and understood that these dreams are a mixture of memories, the reader is somewhat prepared for further breaks in the chronology of the narrative.

Is the transcendence of time and space an actual physical possibility, or is it merely a state of mind? Is it science or mysticism? DeMallie reminds us that, "The distinction between natural and supernatural, so basic to European thought, was meaningless in Lakota culture" (DeMallie 27). Psychoanalyst Carl Jung visited the Pueblo Indians of New Mexico and observed, "The idea, absurd to us, that a ritual act can magically affect the sun is, upon closer examination, no less irrational but far more familiar to us than might at first be assumed. Our Christian religion – like every other, incidentally – is permeated by the idea that special acts…can influence God" (253).

Let us turn to a chapter in Alan's book, *The Sacred Hoop,* called "The Ceremonial Motion of Indian Time: Long Ago, So Far" and read the first two paragraphs:

The traditional tribal concept of time is timelessness, as the concept of space is multidimensionality. In the ceremonial world the tribes inhabit, time and space are mythic.

Years ago Fred Young, the Navajo mathematician and physicist, explained to me the essential movement of time and space. He said that if you held time constant, space went into infinity, and when space was held constant, time moved to infinity. That was why it was not possible to determine the exact location of a particle on a grid. The tribal sense of self as a moving event within a moving universe is very similar to the physicist's understanding of the particle within time and space. (147)

In Native American religion, the catalyst for transcending time is the ceremony; thus, Allen's reference to "ceremonial time." The ceremony prepares the participants, puts them in the right frame of mind, unites them to a single purpose. The ceremony may include consumption of peyote, which induces "euphoria and…a sense of timelessness" (Stewart 3). In James

Morrow's novel, *Galapagos Regained*, fictional characters interact with actual historical figures, including Charles Darwin, Thomas Huxley, Gregor Mendel, Rosalind Franklin, Arthur Schopenhauer, Lucile Swan, and Samuel Wilberforce. The fact that some of these notable individuals were not contemporaries is resolved by a time/space anomaly, localized in a Turkish hookah den, which apparently acts as a hub for historical figures to weave in and out through swirling clouds of cannabis smoke. But the drug factor is not universal to all ceremonies nor is it necessary for transcendence. For example, La Barre says it is doubtful that participants in the Native American Ghost Dance movement of the late 1800s considered peyote essential to their ceremony; instead, just as news about the Ghost Dance spread when previously unacquainted tribes met on reservations and in missionary schools, so did the word spread about peyote. "In the days following the cessation of inter-tribal warfare, peyotism was able to exploit the friendly contacts growing out of the Ghost Dance" (La Barre 112). Morrow explains in an email that he only used the hookah den scenario "because my novel is a celebration of scientific humanism, as opposed to supernatural or theistic arguments about how the universe works, so I wanted to circumscribe the frankly fantastical time-travel element. The scheme of the novel demanded a buffer...between plausible events...and impossible goings-on" (Morrow). When an interviewer asked former Beatle John Lennon about the influence of drugs on songwriting, Lennon said, "The beer and drugs are to prevent the rest of the world from crowding in on you. They don't make you write any better" (McCabe). Tayo and his fellow veterans stay "drunk all the time" (Silko 37) because "Liquor was a medicine for the anger that made them hurt, for the pain of the loss, medicine for tight bellies" (37) but it doesn't cure them. Other aspects of the ceremony that keep the world from crowding in are drumming, dancing, sometimes fasting, burning sage (DeMallie 3), and sweating in a sweat lodge (Looking Horse 71, 72).

Carl Jung highly regarded Neihardt's book, *Black Elk Speaks* (Steltenkamp 95). Jung did not write nearly as much about the Pueblo Indians than he did about alchemy, but some of his writing on alchemy parallels the ontology of American Indians. For example, while chiseling the names of his paternal ancestors on three stone tablets for his garden, Jung became acutely aware of the links between himself and his ancestors, as though he had to complete or continue things which his forebears left unfinished (Jung 232, 233). He writes, "A collective problem, if not recognized as such, always appears as a personal problem, and…may give the impression that something is out of order in the realm of the personal psyche" (233, 234). This has great bearing on the plight of Tayo in *Ceremony*. The traditional medicine man, Ku'oosh, tells Tayo he wants to help him recover from PTSD because, "It is important to all of us. Not only for your sake, but for this fragile world" (Silko 33), and later, "I'm afraid of what will happen to all of us if you and the others don't get well" (35). Tayo and the other war veterans in *Ceremony* are mentally unwell because their psyches are fragmented. Some of the men live in the past, always talking about the women they had while in the military. They drink alcohol to block the bad memories. Tayo cannot reconcile his past and present. In alchemy, Jung discovered the *coniunctio oppositorum*, in which the amalgamation of two elements symbolizes the reconciliation of two parts of a man's soul, or the joining of consciousness to unconsciousness, or the reuniting of man with God (Jung 338).

Jung says it is the *anima* (man's feminine side or woman's masculine side) that communicates images of the unconscious to the conscious mind (187). In *The Sacred Hoop*, Alan asserts that traditional Native American tribal lifestyles "are more often gynocratic than not, and they are never patriarchal" (2). "There is a spirit that pervades everything…Old Spider Woman is one name for this quintessential spirit…Corn Woman…Earth Woman" (13). Through the study of alchemy, Jung discovered the iconic "*kater* (mixing vessel), the vessel of spiritual transformation" and says "the *kater* is a feminine principle which could find no place in Freud's patriarchal world" (Jung 201). In *Ceremony*, Tayo's grandmother represents the quintessential feminine spirt. She knows what to do. Auntie worries about what other people will think if they send for a medicine man. Old Grandma says, "He's my grandson…why do you care what they say?" (31) and when Auntie questions the validity of Betonie's qualifications as medicine man, Grandma says, "Never mind. Old man Ku'oosh knows him, and he thinks this man Betonie might help him." (107). Men performed the ceremony, but it fell upon the Old Grandma to put the cycle in motion.

If we compare the practices and paraphernalia used in the ceremonies of (1) traditional American Indians, as represented by *Ceremony's* Ku'oosh, (2) European alchemists from medieval times through the Renaissance, and (3) the unconventional, forward-thinking medicine man, *Ceremony's* Betonie, we find that they all have at least two references in common: time and space.

Indian paraphernalia includes the eagle feather, "so that the thoughts of men that should rise as high as eagles do" (Neihardt 2); the sacred pipe, or Calumet, "revered as a holy object and as a way for humans to communicate with sacred beings (Sacred Pipe); the rattle and the flute; blue cornmeal (Silko 34); the hides and skull of buffalos; the "morning star…(which) consists of a leather star tinged with blue, and from the center of the star hangs a strip of hide from the breast of a buffalo, together with a feather from the wing of an eagle" (Neihardt xxiii); and the medicine wheel, a great circle of stones on the ground, with a center stone and more stones radiating from the center like spokes of a wheel.

Alchemy is an ancient forerunner to metallurgy and chemistry, but alchemists did not draw a line between science and mysticism as we do today. Numerous Renaissance paintings depict alchemists in their laboratories, surrounded by certain paraphernalia. Most include beakers, retorts, bottles, measuring cups, and furnaces. A painting called *Alchemist* by David Teniers, circa 1651, shows a skull, an hourglass, a globe of earth, pottery, and books. Gerrit Dou's *The Astronomer by Candlelight* includes an hourglass and a globe of the earth. Peter Breughel's *The Alchemist* (1558) also includes an hourglass, as does Adriaen van Ostade's *An Alchemist* (1661), while Joseph Wright's dazzling 1771 painting, *The Discovery of Phosphorus*, shows, not an hourglass but a clock, in the background. The clock is significant when we consider that F. D. Klingender called Wright, "the first professional painter to express the spirit of the Industrial Revolution" (Waterhouse 285). Wright's painting also has a globe as well as a full moon. The hourglasses and clock represent time, of course, and the numerous terrestrial globes represent space, as do the graduated measuring cups and cylinders. By "space" I do not necessarily mean outer space, but space as in place or land, the space on earth in which a person stands and moves around. The measuring cups show the amount of space occupied by liquids and powders, broken down into increments of ounces or milliliters.

Many Native American medicine wheels align with sun, moon, and stars (Scherrer), which alludes to celestial time-keeping and later, navigation. American Indians positioned medicine wheels on the ground, outdoors and open to the sun and sky; conversely, the European alchemists contained time in an hourglass, as grains of sand, measuring how long to heat distillations and mixtures. While the alchemists wanted to control or subdue the elements, and even time itself, American Indians lived in harmony with the elements, as integral elements of the universe.

We now come to Betonie, a different kind of medicine man. When Tayo visited Ku'oosh, the old medicine man "spoke softly, using the old dialect full of sentences that were involuted with explanations of their own origins, as if nothing the old man said were his own but all had been said before and he was only there to repeat it" (Ceremony 31). Ku'oosh recognizes that his medicine is not able to cure Tayo's PTSD, but to his credit, the old man refers Tayo to a more forward-thinking medicine man called Betonie who lives in the nearby town of Gallup. Betonie lives in the foothills above the commercialized Ceremonial Grounds, which is basically a run-down town offering low wages, low-rent rooms, and alleys between saloons where the drunks go to sleep. But once a year, the tourists come to the Ceremonial Grounds and the Indians put on a show for them. Betonie tells Tayo that people wonder why he lives "so closed to this filthy town. But see, this Hogan was here first. Built long before the white people ever came. It is that town down there which is out of place. Not this old medicine man" (109), still another referral to space occupied on the earth. Inside Betonie's home, Tayo smells "a great variety of herb and root odors…almost hidden by the smell of mountain sage…dried desert tea…shrunken skin pouches… painted gourd rattles and deer-hoof clackers of the ceremony" (109 - 111), all of which constitute the more traditional paraphernalia of the medicine man. But besides these items, Tayo notices "the odor of old newspapers and cardboard" (110). He sees a "clutter of boxes and trunks stacked almost to the ceiling beams...Woolworth bags (containing) "bouquets of dried sage and brown leaves of mountain tobacco" (110). He sees bundles of newspapers, piles of telephone books from all over the country, stacks of calendars, and empty iconic Coke bottles. The calendars represent *time*, analogous to the medicine wheels and hourglasses; the phone books represent the *space* occupied by each city.

Silko writes of Betonie's partial explanation, "'In the old days it was simple. A medicine person could get by without all these things. But nowadays...' He let his voice trail off and nodded to let Tayo complete the thought for him" (111). Betonie later says the old ceremonies used to be enough, "But since the white people came, the elements in this world began to shift; it became necessary to create new ceremonies...witchery works to scare people, to make them fear growth...but things that don't shift and grow are dead things" (116).

We should note certain characteristics of Betonie's technique. He lets Tayo make certain connections for himself, as when he trails off in the above sentence. The phone books indicate the bigger world, which Tayo has seen because of his Army experience. The more traditional medicine men are less travelled and work within immediate their surroundings. Betonie says people are always surprised at the places he has travelled (112). Tayo notices that he and Betonie both have hazel-colored eyes. Betonie let's Tayo mention it first, then says, "My grandmother was a remarkable Mexican with green eyes" (109), indicating that he and Tayo are both mixed-bloods. Betonie says people think he is crazy. This is another thing Tayo can relate to, having spent time in the V.A. hospital for psychiatric problems, like when he was convinced that a dead Japanese soldier was his uncle Josiah. Tayo tells Betonie that he recognizes some of the calendars as the same kind that Josiah used to bring home from the Santa Fe depot. Betonie replies, "That gives me some place to start" (111).

Betonie and his helper take Tayo to the top of a mountain and perform a ceremony that involves deftly cutting the top of Tayo's head with a sharp piece of flint and then walking him through a series of five hoops erected near sand paintings. The hoops correspond to a Pueblo Indian myth, an old story told in verse format, which Silko inserts periodically between sections of the narrative text. The story tells of a man transformed into a coyote by a trickster coyote. The man's family follow his tracks, first to a hard oak tree where he had spent one night, next to scrub oak tree where he had spent another night, then to a piñon tree, a juniper, and finally a wild rose bush. They find him suffering from thirst and hunger, trying to talk but only able to make coyote sounds with his voice. To change him back to a man, they go to the old Bear People, who instruct them to make hoops from each type of tree and bush he slept under, with rose twigs, yucca spruce, sage, and other ingredients. The man must pass through these hoops, going back the way he came, and thus become human again. Tayo passes through the hoops while Betonie chants.

Moskowitz writes, "Loop quantum gravity posits that space-time itself is made of quantized, discrete bits, in the form of tiny, one-dimensional loops." Hoops and circles are a common motif in science fiction stories about travelling through time and space. The movie *Contact* (Warner Brothers, 1997), directed by Robert Zemeckis and based on a novel by Carl Sagan, features a large structure resembling a gyroscope made of several revolving metal rings, ostensibly designed by extraterrestrials to transport a person 26 light years away in a matter of seconds. In *Stargate* (MGM, 1994), directed by Roland Emmerich, scientists discover hieroglyphs that refer to constellations and spatial coordinates, which allows them to enter a "wormhole," or short-cut in time, when they walk through a giant upright ring.

After the ceremony, Tayo spends the night on the mountain. When he wakes up the next morning, the mountain is the same, but different. Silko writes, "He remembered the black of the sand paintings on the floor of the Hogan...there were no boundaries; the world below and the sand paintings inside became the same that night. The mountains from all directions had been gathered there that night" (Silko 134, 135).

19

Betonie tells Tayo that the ceremony is not finished yet, but that he has had a vision:

(Betonie) was drawing in the dirt with his fingers. "Remember these stars," he said. "I've seen (the stars) and I've seen spotted cattle; I've seen a mountain and I've seen a woman."

Tayo pursues the vision described by Betonie, rounding up his Uncle Josiah's spotted cattle. Along the way, he meets a woman who invites him into her house and feeds him. "The sky is clear," she says. "You can see the stars tonight" (165). When he looks outside at the sky, he sees the stars are exactly as Betonie had drawn with his fingers in the dirt. Tayo and the woman make love. She is the woman in Betonie's vision and he will meet her again later to spend a blissful summer together.

Hunting for the cattle takes Tayo's mind off his troubled past. He is no longer sick to his stomach:

The silence was inside, in his belly; there was no longer any hurry. The ride into the mountain had branched into all directions of time. He knew why the oldtimers could only speak of yesterday and tomorrow in terms of the present moment: the only certainty; and this present sense of being was qualified with bare hints of yesterday or tomorrow, by saying "I go up to the mountain yesterday or I go up to the mountain tomorrow." The ck'o'yo Kaup'a'ta somewhere is stacking his gambling sticks and waiting for a visitor; Rocky [who died in the war] and I are walking across the ridge in the moonlight; Josiah and Robert are waiting for us. This night is a single night; and there has never been any other. (179)

Quantum scientist have demonstrated that the same atom can occupy two spaces at once (Aron), which brings us full circle to the beginning of this essay and the power of words. Einstein's famous words "energy equals mass times the speed of light squared," or $E=MC^2$, have become synonymous with atomic energy, including the invention of the atomic bomb, which plays a pivotal role in Silko's *Ceremony*. But Einstein's only direct involvement with the atomic bomb was his signature on a letter to President Franklin Roosevelt, drafted by Leo Szilard and Eugene Wigner in 1939, urging the President to consider the military applications of atomic energy (Eugene Wigner). Einstein's real interest was on the interaction between time and space, not the "witchery" that Tayo finally recognizes, "where they exploded the first atomic bomb...and the top-secret laboratories where the bomb was had been created...deep in the Jemez Mountains, on land the Government took from Cochiti Pueblo: Los Alamos, only a hundred miles northeast of (Tayo) now...the point of convergence...he recognized why the Japanese voices had merged with Laguna voices...the lines of cultures and worlds were drawn in flat dark lines on fine light sand, converging in the middle of witchery's final ceremonial sand painting" (Silko 228) and Tayo's ceremony is complete when he realizes that with the advent of the atom bomb, "human beings were one clan again, united by the fate the destroyers planned for all of them" (228).

Ideally, Tayo is right about all humans belonging to one clan, but we know that words and ceremonies can manipulate this reality. It works both ways. The Naturalization Ceremony is one example. "If USCIS approves your Form N-400, Application for Naturalization, we will schedule you to take the Oath of Allegiance at a naturalization ceremony. Taking the oath will complete the process of becoming a U.S. citizen" (USCIS). Conversely, a person can become *stateless* when "not considered as a national by any state under operation of law" (UNHCR). "Under operation of law" implies a set of words, spoken in a context, or ceremony, which gives power to those words. When anyone speaks the Oath of Allegiance in a naturalization ceremony, or is declared a non-citizen in the land of their birth, that person becomes, like Tayo's mountain, the same but different.

Works Cited

Allen, Paula Gunn. *The Sacred Hoop: Recovering the Feminine in American Indian Traditions*. Beacon, 1992.

Aron, Jacob. "New quantum record as ball of atoms ends up in two spots at once." 28 December 2015. *New Scientist*. https://www.newscientist.com/article/dn28709-new-quantum-record-as-ball-of-atoms-ends-up-in-two-spots-at-once/. Accessed 20 April 2019.

DeMallie, Raymond J. "Lakota Belief and Ritual in the Nineteenth Century." *Sioux Indian Religion: Tradition and Innovation*. Edited by Raymond J. DeMallie and Douglas R. Parks. University of Oklahoma Press, Norman, 1987.

"Eugene Wigner: American Physicist." *Encyclopedia Britannica Online*. https://www.britannica.com/biography/Eugene-Wigner#ref124710. Accessed 6 April 2019.

Jung, Carl G. *Memories, Dreams, Reflections*. Vintage Books/Random House, 1989.

Looking Horse, Arval. *Sioux Indian Religion: Tradition and Innovation*. Edited by Raymond J. DeMallie and Douglas R. Parks. University of Oklahoma Press, 1989.

Momaday, N. Scott. *The Man Made of Words*. St. Martin's Griffin, 1998.

Moskowitz, Clara. "Spece-Time Loops May Explain Black Holes." 10 July 2013. *SPACE.com*. Accessed 22 April 2019.

Neihardt, John G. *Black Elk Speaks: The Complete Edition*. University of Nebraska Press, 2014.

"Sacred Pipe." *Encyclopedia Britannica Online*.

https://www.britannica.com/topic/Sacred-Pipe. Accessed 6 April 2019.

Scherrer, Deborah. "Medicine Wheels and Cultural Connections." *Stanford University.* http://solar-center.stanford.edu/AO/Medicine-Wheels.pdf. Accessed 7 April 2019.

Steltenkamp, Michael F. *Black Elk: Holy Man of the Oglala.* University of Oklahoma Press, 1997.
Stewart, Omer C. *Peyote Religion: A History (Civilization of the American Indian Series).* University of Oklahoma Press, 1987.

McCabe, Peter and Robert Schonfeld. "John and Yoko Interview." September 5th, 1971. *Penthouse Magazine.* Penthouse International, 1984. Retrieved from *The Beatles Interview Database.* http://www.beatlesinterviews.org/db1971.0905.beatles.html. Accessed 3 April 2019.

Morrow, James. "Re: Hookah Den in Galapagos Regained." Received by Bill Ectric, 16 April 2019.

UNHCR. UN High Commissioner for Refugees. *The 1954 Convention relating to the Status of Stateless Persons: Implementation within the European Union Member States and Recommendations for Harmonisation.* October 2003. https://www.refworld.org/docid/415c3cfb4.html. Accessed 23 April 2019.

USCIS. U.S. Citizenship and Immigration Services. Department of Homeland Security. Federal Government of the United States.

Waterhouse, Ellis. *Painting in Britain 1530 to 1790.* Viking Penguin, 1978.

A section of *The Apotheosis of George Washington*, Herculaneum Pottery, c. 1800-1805, John James Barralet, artist.

Daderot, CC0, via Wikimedia Commons

My Summer Twin

I was born in June,
Far as can be from December's gray.
I soared through valiant summers
in slow motion leaps and bounds,
the great joyful sun ball rolling
over, under, and around me
like the science teacher's shiny mobile.

My Gemini girl
had lustrous hair that bounced
with each seesaw lift and dive.
She held my hand when, inevitably,
a bee sting introduced us to terror.

1966

One of my magic years is 1966. My 12th birthday was in June of that year. Sociologists and psychologists describe the ages of 12 to 14 as early adolescence, the onset of puberty, the ability to form more complex thoughts, and a moving away from parents in search of individuality.

1966 felt like I was on the cusp of something new, something wild, maybe even weird. Images filtered into our home via magazines, television, and film – images of Andy Warhol's Exploding Plastic Inevitable, featuring The Velvet Underground and Nico, for example. I didn't know what it all meant, but it was something not for the parents. We could buy cool wrap-around sunglasses, similar to the ones worn by members of the Velvet Underground.

Of course, there were other good years after 1966, and in real life you can't really draw a line between years; one blends into the other. But 1966 was the last year I could truly enjoy the tactile, glittering combination of plastic, electronics, sugar (on cereal, in bubble gum and Coca-Cola), and unlimited potential, without the teenage angst, the far-off dread of the Vietnam war, new pressures of school, and the guilt imposed by environmentalists. Don't get me wrong – I want to save the planet – but I'm just talking about the way I felt as a kid. After the 1967 Summer of Love, plastic became a derogatory word for fake and hypocritical, and it was ruining our planet because plastic is not biodegradable. The hippie communes fascinated me. I read Thoreau's Walden and briefly considered a hermit's life in a cabin in the woods. It never would have worked. Even camping out in the backyard with my friends had drawbacks. It got cold at three o'clock in the morning!

I know it sounds strange that a twelve-year-old would be worried about going to war. I should explain that in my small town, 1966 seemed to last until 1969. By 1969, the '67 Summer of Love had given way to what some called "the death of the American Dream," or "America's loss of innocence," with events like the Sharon Tate murders and the killing of a concertgoer by the Hell's Angels at a Rolling Stones concert in Altamont. In one of my favorite book passages of all time, Hunter S. Thompson's *Fear and Loathing in Las Vegas* (1972), subtitled, *A Savage Journey Into the Heart of the American Dream*, writes about the great wave of sixties hope finally breaking and rolling back:

> We had all the momentum; we were riding the crest of a high and beautiful wave. . .So now, less than five years later, you can go up on a steep hill in Las Vegas and look West, and with the right kind of eyes you can almost see the high-water mark—that place where the wave finally broke and rolled back. —Hunter S. Thompson, *Fear and Loathing In Las Vegas* (1972, Random House

In the April 8, 1966 issue of *Time Magazine*, John T. Elson wrote the cover story, "Is God Dead?" It was an even-handed look backward and forward about the questions of faith and doctrines. You might say it formed my theology because we didn't go to church when I was growing up. My mother used to read things to the rest of our family in a kind of conversational, "oh-this-is-interesting" way. I think it was her way of teaching my brother and I things, which she didn't know how to put into her own words, knowing we could read it for ourselves but probably wouldn't. I remember her reading excerpts from the *Time* magazine article, like where Elson said,

"Protestant faith now means not intellectual acceptance of an ancient confession, but open commitment—perhaps best symbolized in the U.S. by the civil rights movement—to eradicating the evil and inequality that beset the world," and "In search of meaning, some believers have desperately turned to psychiatry, Zen or drugs. Thousands of others have quietly abandoned all but token allegiance to the churches, surrendering themselves to a life of 'anonymous Christianity' dedicated to civil rights or the Peace Corps" (John Elson, *Time Magazine*, April 8, 1966). Now I attend services at Saint John's Cathedral, an Episcopalian church that specializes in feeding the hungry and housing the homeless.

The luxury of being twelve years old in 1966 is that I felt as though I had plenty of time to figure out religion. In 1966, we were a household of smiles, laughter, my brother's first bicycle, with butterfly handlebars and a banana seat; my first camera, a Kodak Brownie 127 model; our family's first combination record player/8-Track tape stereo. My father taught my brother and me to solder wires and helped me build a crystal radio from a kit. We hooked up a plastic skull to a small motor and put it in a cabinet. When you opened the cabinet, the skull opened its mouth and a little tape recorder said, "Oh, my aching bones" or "Why are you looking in here?" or anything else we recorded on the three-inch reel of tape.

Ford Motor Company introduced eight-track tape players in three of its 1966 models: Mustang, Thunderbird, and Lincoln. RCA Victor introduced 175 Stereo-8 Cartridges from its music catalog.1966 media landmarks, for me, include:

The Jeff Beck/Jimmy Page version of the Yardbirds, who, along with

Keith Relf, Jim McCarty, and Chris Dreja, had a cameo appearance in Michelangelo Antonioni's film *Blow-Up* (1966). Film critic Andrew Sarris called the film "a mod masterpiece." *Blow-Up* reflected sights, sounds, and mood of "Swinging London." In the *New York Times*, Bosley Crowther called the movie a "fascinating picture, which has something real to say about the matter of personal involvement and emotional commitment in a jazzed-up, media-hooked-in world so cluttered with synthetic stimulations that natural feelings are overwhelmed." Fuzz-tone guitar electronics was getting more popular.

If I had to pick a favorite Beatles album, I would choose their 7th studio album, *Revolver*, released on August 5, 1966, a marriage of philosophy, romance, and rock & roll. Revolver embodies a perfect balance of exuberant summer warmth, autumn-like Gothic melancholy, and meditative psychedelia, driven by whip-snap drumming, hot ringing guitar tones, and the drone of Hindustani classical music. My verdant valiant summer took on a pleasant chill as leaves began to ripen and die, while I, like a grinning glow-skull, reveled in the profound implications of getting stronger while simultaneously aging in time and place, living outside of time looking in, knowing I could always return to this window of scrutiny at any age. Lennon and Harrison, in particular, were experimenting with LSD. McCartney was experimenting with avant-garde techniques like musique concrète. Starr's top-notch drumming held it all together. One need only listen to the plodding, wobbling outtake of Tomorrow Never Knows on the Beatles' Anthology Album to appreciate Starr's dynamic drumming on the superior *Revolver* version.

Truman Capote described his book, *In Cold Blood* (Random House, 1966) as a "nonfiction novel." He also called it an "experiment in journalistic writing." This style of writing would come to be known as "New Journalism." Traditional journalism is objective, concerned only with the facts. New Journalism is subjective and includes the author's personal reaction to the subject they are writing about. The writers of New Journalism often insert themselves into the story. Hunter S. Thompson's first published book, *Hell's Angels: The Strange and Terrible Saga of the Outlaw Motorcycle Gangs* (Random House, 1966) is also considered a category of New Journalism called Gonzo. Other New Journalism writers include Tom Wolfe, Norman Mailer, Joan Didion, Terry Southern, Robert Christgau, Gay Talese, and others. According to literary critic Seymour Krim, the term New Journalism was first used in 1965 by Pete Hamill.

Television shows *Star Trek* (NBC), *Dark Shadows* (ABC), *The Monkees* (NBC), *Batman* (ABC), *Mission: Impossible* (CBS) all debuted in 1966. *The Hollywood Squares* (NBC) pilot episode aired in 1965, but the regular series began in 1966. On weekdays, when not in school for whatever reason, I enjoyed watching *Hollywood Squares* with my mother because it brought nine guest celebrities together in one place to display their knowledge and practice their shtick. Also in 1966, The Marvel Super Heroes animated series marked the first appearance of Marvel Comics characters on television. The show was syndicated to local TV stations, independent of the major networks. My friends and I were excited to see Iron Man, Captain America, The Hulk, Thor, and the Submariner on the tube, but disappointed by the low-budget animation, which usually involved still pictures with just the mouths moving when the characters spoke.

Singer Johnny Rivers had a 1966 hit record with *Secret Agent Man*, a song written by P. F. Sloan and Steve Barri. A short version of Secret Agent Man rocked the opening credits *Secret Agent*, a television series starring Patrick McGoohan. This series originally aired in England as *Danger Man* beginning in 1960 with a different theme song (actually two theme songs: first, The *Danger Man Theme*, and later, High Wire, both composed by Edwin Astley). During the sixties "spy craze" ignited by the popularity of James Bond, *Danger Man* came to American television as *Secret Agent*, with the Johnny Rivers song.

Speaking of Patrick McGoohan, his career move in the sixties illustrates a perfect analogy of what I like to call the "1966 transition." *Danger Man*, especially the early episodes, reflected the traditional image of a spy wearing a suit and tie; it harkens back to the 1950s, invoking the cold war and international espionage. Eventually, the series introduced a few spy gadgets as a nod to the James Bond films. McGoohan quit *Danger Man* in 1965 and spent 1966 planning and producing *The Prisoner*. During this time, he obviously had his hand on the pulse of popular culture. *The Prisoner* debuted in 1967. Filmed in the enchanting, storybook-inspired village of Portmeirion in North Wales, The Prisoner reveled in surreal imagery and counterculture rebellion against dubious authority. The dubious authorities subjected the title character (McGoohan) to mind control techniques, including hallucinogenic drugs and dream manipulation. Instead of traditional suits, the characters wore toned-down version of the mod designs found in Swinging England's Carnaby Street. If a prisoner escaped from the island by boat or swimming, a giant bubble chased them down, skimming across the ocean surface, and returned them to captivity. The bubble added an element of science fiction to T*he Prisoner.*

Speaking of science fiction (or was it nonfiction?), *Look Magazine* featured a story in their October 4, 1966 issue called "Aboard a Flying Saucer: The Incredible Story of Two People Who Believe They Were Kidnapped by Humanoids in a Spacecraft." This was the story of Barney and Betty Hill, a real-life couple who claimed to have been abducted by a flying saucer. The Look article consisted of excerpts from the best-selling book, *The Interrupted Journey* (1966, The Dial Press), as told to John G. Fuller by the Hills. The book was made into a television movie called *The UFO Incident* in 1975, starring James Earl Jones and Estelle Parsons. The book is a major source of all the "experimental probing" tropes that are so common today. On some nights I could have sworn I heard weird electric buzzing in the walls and saw unexplained lights in the sky. Incidentally, *Look Magazine's* advertising revenue peaked in 1966 at $80 million. I'm reminded of Ray Palmer, editor of *Amazing Stories* magazine in the 1940s, who said *Amazing Stories* sales increased dramatically when he published a series of stories by Richard Shaver, known collectively as The Shaver

Mystery. Shaver claimed that space aliens, left behind on Earth many years in the past, had evil mutated descendants still living underground in caverns. These mutants would sometimes emerge from their lairs to kidnap humans for nefarious purposes, and they frequently tampered with Shaver's mind by sending invisible rays into his brain. The strangest part of this narrative is that Shaver sincerely claimed that his stories were true.

Two strange things happened to me in 1966. I dreamed I was riding my bicycle and saw a bag of bones on the side of the road. The next day, my brother and I were riding our bicycles with our friend, Dennis, and we actually saw a dirty burlap bag on the side of the road. I lifted the opening of the bag with a stick and there were bones inside! I think they were pig bones from a butcher shop, but still, it was weird. I told my parents about it. My dad said I had probably ridden past it the day before and it registered in my subconscious mind, but I don't think so.

Another thing that happened was an example of *synchronicity*, but I had never heard the word 'synchronicity' back then. The singing duo, Simon and Garfunkel, released an album in October called *Parsley, Sage, Rosemary, and Thyme.* My mother bought the album. Some college students were involved in a contest called a scavenger hunt, in which they had to go around from house to house asking for various items on a list. Whoever collected all the items won some kind of prize for their sorority or fraternity. Items like a 1964 penny, a pencil with the name of a business on it and so on. Two girls knocked on our door with four sheets of paper and a roll of scotch tape. They needed a small bit of four different spices or herbs to tape to each piece of paper. The four items had to be parsley, sage, rosemary, and thyme, because the Simon and Garfunkel album was so popular among college students. My mother was happy to help them out while my brother and I looked on. She had parsley, sage, and thyme, but no rosemary. The college girls were disappointed, of course.

My eight-year-old brother asked me, "What kind of spice is in that tea bag in your Bible?"

"What are you talking about?" I asked.

My aunt had given me a Bible for my 12th birthday, but I didn't know anything about a tea bag. My brother went into my room and found the Bible where I had left it, unread, on a shelf. It was one of those big Bibles with a soft leather cover and pages so supple you could place a small object in it with barely a bulge. Sure enough, when we looked in the Bible, there was a flattened little cloth bag with some kind of powdered herb in it.

"I don't think it's a tea bag," said my mother. She held it up to her nose. "It smells like rosemary – it IS rosemary!"

The college girls jumped up and down and laughed with glee. One of the college girls was studying parapsychology and said that packets of rosemary were used as good luck charms. They taped a little bit of each spice to a piece of paper.

"Thank you all so much!" they said and were on their way.

We called my aunt and she said she didn't put the packet of rosemary in my Bible. I accused my brother of doing it. My mother accused me of it. My dad said it didn't matter who did it, but that it would have been luckier if it was a tea bag because then at least we could drink it.

Bill's Bookshelf # 1
The Midnight People
1968, Popular Library Edition, Leslie Frewin Publishers Limited
Edited by Peter Haining

I bought this book, brand new off the shelf for 75 cents, in 1968 or 1969, when I was approximately 14 years oldr. While *The Midnight People* is ostensibly a vampire anthology, Editor Peter Haining chose to include a couple of stories in which the vampire tag is debatable. The book is stronger for those choices, however.

The cover features a painting by <u>Hieronymus Bosch </u>called Death and the Usurer, also known as Death of the Miser.

This is an almost perfect example of the kind of books I loved to pore over when I was a kind, reading not only the stories and introductions, but also the front material, which included a list of when and where the stories first appeared (usually magazines), with copyright information and so on. The only reason this is not the perfect example of my collection is that it does not include the list of sources. Of course, that's no problem, now that we have the internet.

After the Introduction, the collection begins with an article by Montague Summers (1880 – 1948) about real-life German serial killer <u>Fritz Haarmann </u>(1879 – 1925), who was known as "The Hanover Vampire" because he actually murdered his victims by biting into their throats.

Montague Summers was a strange character himself. He studied theology at Oxford, became a Deacon in the Church of England, but later

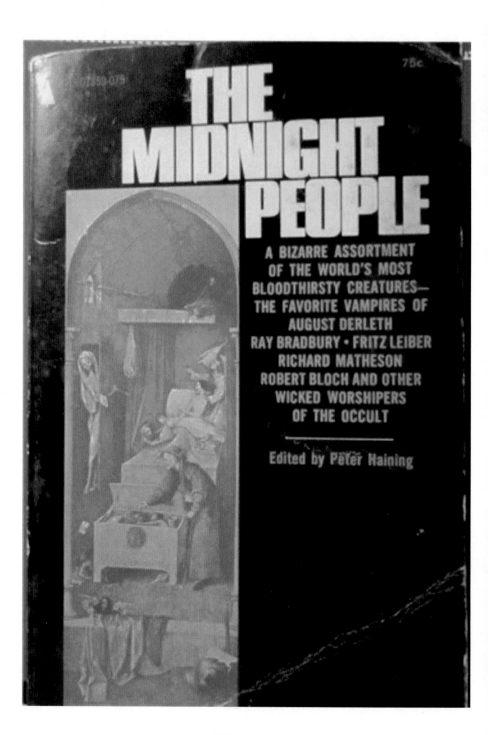

THE MIDNIGHT PEOPLE

A BIZARRE ASSORTMENT
OF THE WORLD'S MOST
BLOODTHIRSTY CREATURES—
THE FAVORITE VAMPIRES OF
AUGUST DERLETH
RAY BRADBURY • FRITZ LEIBER
RICHARD MATHESON
ROBERT BLOCH AND OTHER
WICKED WORSHIPERS
OF THE OCCULT

Edited by Peter Haining

75c

converted to Catholicism and gave himself the title of Reverend, although historians have found no evidence that the Catholic Church officially ordained him as a priest. Summers had peculiar interests, ranging from occult (vampires, werewolves, and witches) to deviant sexual practices (the Marquis de Sade and the Greek chronicles of Antinous and Hadrian). In 1928, Summers published the first English translation of Heinrich Kramer's 1486 treatise on witchcraft, *Malleus Maleficarum* (Hammer of the Witches).

The Midnight People includes the M. R. James story, *An Episode of Cathedral History*, which is one of my favorite supernatural stories, combining, as it does, James' vague but chilling depiction of an undead thing escaping from a tomb under a church, with a storyline that literally defines the gothic horror genre. "It was in 1840 that the wave of the Gothic revival smote the Cathedral of Southminster," says the old church caretaker, Mr. Worby, referring to the 19th Century fashion trend of restoring authentic gothic structures and by building new structures in a mock Gothic style. Worby explains that a church official, intent on having a Gothic style cathedral, ordered carpenters to remove most of the sanctuary's beautiful handcrafted woodwork, including the podium, under which was discovered a stone slab that sealed the mysterious tomb.

Most people know the story of how John Polidori wrote *The Vampyre* as the result of a challenge by Lord Byron to a small circle of friends, which included Mary and Percy Shelley, to each write a ghost story. Mary Shelley eventually wrote *Frankenstein* (1818) as a result of that challenge, and Polidori wrote *The Vampyre* (1819). This was not the first vampire story ever written, but it was probably the first one written in English, and it set the now-familiar image of the vampire as aristocrat – a cloaked lord or nobleman, Byronic, decadent, and darkly romantic.

Editor Peter Haining tells us that *Bat's Belfry* is one of August Derleth's first horror stories, containing "certain elementary mistakes which can be expected from any young writer." This is a whopping understatement. It's a silly hodge-podge of supernatural motifs. I should add that I greatly admire Mr. Derleth for his industrious achievement, along with Donald Wandrei, of establishing Arkham House Publishers, a classic "weird fiction" small press success story.

"...those holy men, with the white garments of
the angel, pretending to read books, and yet all the
time their eyes never on the page, and all of us with the
bowed head. And all for what? She is dead, so! Is it
not?" – Van Helsing to Dr. Seward, Chapter 13,
Dracula by Bram Stoker

The potential for deconstruction looms in the text of Bram Stoker's
Dracula like bright red eyes in the London fog. Why deconstruction? Early in
the story, describing his journey from England to Transylvania, Jonathan
Harker writes in his journal, "The impression I had was that we were leaving
the West and entering the East" (Stoker). The significance of Harker's

observation, in the context of this paper, is that Western thought rests upon Platonic concepts that Jacques Derrida famously deconstructed. Plato, expanding on the teachings of Socrates, is generally credited with "laying the foundations of Western philosophy and science" (Encyclopædia Britannica), so Harker's sensation of "leaving the West" indicates a strange trip into Eastern mysticism for him, an Englander.

On his way from England to Transylvania, Jonathan Harker writes in his journal, "Beyond the green swelling hills of the Mittel Land rose mighty slopes of forest up to the lofty steeps of the Carpathians themselves" (Stoker 7). The Mittel Land, or "middle land," is the space between West (England) and East (Transylvania). In that moment, Harker exists between binary opposites. At this juncture, Harker faces a crucial choice: Continue to Dracula's castle or return home. Either choice will be literally and inescapably irrational, thereby illustrating Derrida's observations on Kierkegaard's statement, "The instant of decision is madness" (Derrida 66). The reason a decision is "madness" is that if we must decide something, we don't have a clear indication of a pro that outweighs a con. If the choice was obvious, we wouldn't have to decide; the decision would present itself. Therefore, at the point of decision, it is a leap of faith. Jonathan Harker's instinct for survival is aroused, first by weird dreams and dogs howling all night, to the villager's pitying looks and thinly veiled fear of Dracula and the peasant woman's urgent warnings to turn back, until he writes, "I am not feeling nearly as easy in my mind as usual" (5) and soon, "had there been any alternative I should have taken it" (9), and finally, "I felt a sort of paralysis of fear" (10). But on the other hand, Harker reminds himself, "I am now a full-blown solicitor!" (11) and he remembers his duty to his employer. To turn back would be to botch his assignment, and maybe even to lose his position with the law firm. Should he continue to Dracula's castle despite his desperate sense of mortal danger, or fail in the job for which he has worked so hard to obtain? This is truly an irrational decision no matter what he chooses.

Derrida says western thought is made up largely of binary opposites: man/woman, spirit/matter, nature/culture, speaking/writing, civilized/primitive and so forth, and that we tend to privilege one part of a binary pair as superior to the other part, often without realizing we are doing it. Examining binary oppositions to words and concepts in a text can reveal the inner contradictions of a text. Words are defined, at least in part, by what

40

they are not. For example, the definition of *man* is "not woman," so the word *man* has a transient vanishing *trace* of the word *woman*. Derrida seems to enjoy ghostly references. Peim describes Derrida's theory of the spectre as "a variation on the positions established in his earlier works on the trace," so it seems fitting here to recall the passage in Dracula in which Harker writes, "Once there appeared a strange optical effect. When he stood between me and the flame he did not obstruct it, for I could see its ghostly flicker all the same. This startled me, but as the effect was only momentary, I took it that my eyes deceived me straining through the darkness." Like the glimpses of meaning manifested by binary opposites. When Harker returns to civilization, recuperating from a nervous breakdown in a sanitarium, his nurse writes to his fiancé that "The *traces* of such an illness as his do not lightly die away" (64, italics mine).

The text of *Dracula* includes comparisons of West to East in terms of topography and inhabitants, using such binary opposites as urban/rural, civilized/wild, and modern/primitive. The assumption that the West is a better place to live, with its modern technology and civilized citizens, is inferred by the author, as well as the various characters who narrate the story, and most probably even by us, the readers of the novel. Harker says, "It seems to me that the further east you go the more unpunctual are the trains. What ought they to be in China?" (Stoker 4) and "I read that every known superstition in the world is gathered into the horseshoe of the Carpathians" (3). Harker is condescending in his description of the peasants' clothing, saying that the peasant women "looked pretty, except when you got near them, but they were very clumsy about the waist" (4). The Spanish translation of Dracula says, "they were pretty thick around the waist." In 1897, when Stoker wrote Dracula, respectable Victorian women wore corsets. Stepanic reminds us that "The small waist was a marker of Victorian beauty" and that when Harker describes the Slovaks as "charming with tall boots and dashing mustaches…but wanting in natural self-assertion (Stoker 4)," the implication is that the Slovaks are "unlike Harker, who lets nothing interfere with his duties to his employer" (Stepanic).

Glib as Harker may be about the peasants' clothing and manner, it is a peasant woman who unselfishly gives him the gift of a crucifix for his protection and begs him to avoid Dracula's castle. She asks nothing in return. Much later in the book, when Harker is tracking the destinations of Dracula's boxes of earth, and in contrast to the peasant woman's sincerity and generosity, every dockworker and freight handler in London wants recompense in the form of money or alcohol for answering the least of Harker's inquiries. Increasingly humorous passages found in Chapters 17 and 20 outline the progression of Harker's search for Dracula's cargo. At his first stop, the freight men emphasize that:

> the boxes were `main and mortal heavy', and that shifting them was dry work. One of them added that it was hard lines that there wasn't any gentleman `such like as like yourself, squire', to show some sort of appreciation of their efforts in a liquid form. Another put in a rider that the thirst then generated was such that even the time which had elapsed had not completely allayed it. Needless to add, I took care before leaving to lift, forever and adequately, this source of reproach (Stoker 141).

His second stop is King's Cross, where:

> The opportunities of acquiring an abnormal thirst had been here limited. A noble use of them had, however, been made, and again I was compelled to deal with the result in ex post facto manner (141, 142).

Then to on to the next establishment, where:

> The carriers' men were able to supplement the paucity of the written words with a few more details...connected almost solely with the dusty nature of the job, and the consequent thirst engendered in the operators. On my affording an opportunity, through the medium of the currency of the realm, of the allaying, at a later period, this beneficial evil... (142).

And finally, visiting the last freight man's house, Harker finds:

> The very prospect of beer which my expected coming had opened to him had proved too much, and he had begun too early on his expected debauch (162).

According to William Hughes, "It appears that, whatever his personal politics, (Stoker) adopted a solidly conservative stance in debate" and saw himself socially as "solidly within an integrated United Kingdom" (Hughes), so when Van Helsing arrives in London and remarks that "the smuts [soot] of London were not quite so bad as they used to be when he was a student here" ( ) the statement seems, at first glance, like a positive outlook on the improvements London of Bram Stoker's 1890s. But if we read between the binary opposites, "smut...not so bad" reveals a trace of "smut...bad" in the sense that the smut is lessened but still makes its presence known. In fact, "A scientific study of urban fog published in 1896 noted: 'Town fog is mist made white by Nature and painted any tint from yellow to black by her children...contaminated by man with every imaginable abomination'" (Corton). To be "not as bad" is still somewhat bad. The technology of coal furnaces was detrimental to life in London. The further we get from London, the pristine the topography. In a letter, Mina describes the rural town of Whitby, England as having a "beautifully green" valley, and an outlook near a parish church, which, in spite of the gravestones,

> is to my mind the nicest spot in Whitby, for it lies right over the town, and has a full view of the harbour and all up the bay to where the headland called Kettleness stretches out into the sea" ( ) and the setting sun throws red light "over on the East Cliff and the old abbey...to bathe everything in a beautiful rosy glow ( ).

Even further away, in the Carpathian Mountains near Transylvania, Harker beholds a land even less spoiled by civilization:

> a green sloping land full of forests and woods, with here and there steep hills, crowned with clumps of trees or with farmhouses, the blank gable end to the road. There was everywhere a bewildering mass of fruit blossom-- apple, plum, pear, cherry. And as we drove by I could see the green grass under the trees spangled with the fallen petals ( ).

While probably not consciously intended, Stoker's descriptions of the people and topography of wild, rural Carpathia, compared to the people and topography of urban London, reveal a moral an aesthetic privilege favoring the rural, "uncivilized" provinces over the mighty city of London.

Works Cited

Auerbach, Nina and David Skal, editors, Dracula, Norton Critical Edition, 1997, pp. 363–4.

Buzwell, Greg. "Dracula: Vampires, Perversity and Victorian Anxieties." The British Library: Discovering Literature. 15 May 2017. Web. https://www.bl.uk/romantics-and-victorians/articles/dracula. Accessed 5 Oct. 2018 https://www.victoriansecrets.co.uk/bram-stoker/. Accessed 4 November 2018.

"Can Philosophy Free Itself from the Prison of Language?" DerridaTheMovie, 2018. Web. http://www.derridathemovie.com/can-philosophy-free-itself-from-the-prison-of-language/ Accessed 21 October 2018

Corton, Christine. London Fog: The Biography. The Belknap Press of Harvard University Press 2015.

James, M. R. Complete Ghost Stories. Macmillan Collector's Library, Kindle Edition, 2017

Ghai, Samantha. "Modernity in Bram Stoker's Dracual." Chrysalis. 10 Feb. 2017. https://chrysalis17.com/2017/02/10/modernity-in-bram-stokers-dracula/. Accessed 23 November 2018.

Gross, Elizabeth. Derrida and the Limits of Philosophy (Sage Publications, Thesis Eleven, 1986; 14; 26

Hughes, William. "Bram Stoker Introduction." Victorian Secrets. Dec. 1996. Web.

Norton Anthology of English Literature Topics Online. W.W. Norton and Company. https://www.wwnorton.com/college/english/nael/romantic/topic_2/welcome.htm. Accessed 23 November 2018.

Peim, Nick. Spectral Bodies: Derrida and the Philosophy of the Photograph as Historical Document. Wiley Online Library, 29 April 2005. Web.

Stepanic, Stanley. "Dracula Study Guide." Course Hero. 28 Nov. 2016. Web. www.coursehero.com/lit/Dracula. Accessed 4 Nov. 2018

Stoker, Bram. Dracula (Wisehouse Classics - The Original 1897 Edition) . Wisehouse. Kindle Edition.

Teachersage. "In Dracula, what is the significance of the title?" eNotes, 16 July 2008, https://www.enotes.com/homework-help/am-not-sure-what-significance-title-dracula-any-27541. Accessed 23 Nov. 2018.

The Old Lady at the Cantina

Above: Rota, Spain, 1974

I don't know how the Navy does it now, but in 1974, at the Naval Air Station in Rota, Spain, they never drug-tested us. Enhanced by Moroccan hashish, Jim's dark barracks room acquired the paradoxical trappings of an alchemist's laboratory aboard a spacecraft. Loud, mind-altering music from Uriah Heep's *Magician's Birthday* washed over us from big JBL speakers as Jim adjusted the mid-range on his brand-new Marantz amplifier. The amp's beady red power light and blue-glow VU meter suggested a futuristic instrument

47

panel. A wooden cable spool, turned sideways to serve as a table, displayed wine bottles covered with multi-colored layers of melted candle wax, a skull incense burner, a bronze mortar and pestle from Tangier, Morocco, and an assortment of other paraphernalia. Two black light posters fluoresced radiantly: An outer space scene with stars and planets, and a medieval castle in swirling mist. Mesmerized by the lights on the stereo equipment, I told myself I would someday write about it.

Jim could get away with the non-regulation décor in his room because he was a hospital corpsman. Most of us had to undergo periodic room inspections, but the Commander of the Base Hospital decided that because his corpsman worked all hours at a vital job, they deserved some leeway. They never had room inspections.

Uriah Heep were well into the ten-minute opus for which they had named the *Magician's Birthday* album. My stoned brain associated this part of the song with Hall of the Mountain King and the Wicked Witch's oh-eee-oh soldier guards in The Wizard of Oz.

"I bought all this at the Air Force base in Morón de la Frontera," Jim shouted over the music, indicating his stereo system. "It's about 90 miles from here, and they have better prices, better equipment."

"Is that when you met the old palm reader?" I asked.

"Yeah, about halfway to Morón we stopped at a cantina. I bought that mortar and pestle from her, along with this little suerte packet of spices."

"What kind of packet?"

"Suerte. It means luck."

"Like a good luck charm," I said.

"Exactly. She wanted to read my palm, but I was in a hurry. You should go with us this Saturday."

The following Saturday, our friend Buddy Beckler, aircraft mechanic, picked up Jim and me in his rusty orange 1968 Volkswagen Squareback, a squat little station wagon. With Buddy at the wheel, the three of us left the Rota in route to the Morón Air force base. In high spirits, I might add.

Thirty-five minutes into the rural countryside, the cantina loomed into view on the right side of the road, white stucco walls trimmed with bright ceramic tiles of blue, green, and tan. The elderly Spanish woman wore a black mourning dress and bonnet, but no vail. She had a table set up outside the cantina, selling bronze items like candlesticks, statuettes, incense holders, and other stuff. The old lady was assisted by a younger woman, maybe twenty-something. I saw them holding hands under the table and thought, maybe the old woman is her grandmother.

"First," said Jim, "let's quench our thirst."

Inside the cantina, at Jim's recommendation, we asked the bartender for some chilled Oloroso sherry, served up in three large schooner glasses.

"I'm not much of a wine or sherry drinker," said Buddy, "but this is delicious!"

The Oloroso had a nice toasted fruit flavor and high alcohol content. We asked for three more glasses of the stuff and I was feeling good. Having worked for years in a drinking establishment located between two military bases, the bartender spoke good English.

Jim asked him, "Tell us about the woman who sells the bronze."

The bartender wiped his hands on his apron and leaned in as though speaking confidentially and told a gruesome tale. Maybe he wanted to entertain us, so we would keep on buying drinks, but he seemed sincere. He told us that the old woman's name was Señora Graciela de Malaga. She was supposedly descended from the wealthy Heredia family of Malaga. Manuel Agustin Heredia started an iron foundry in the 1820s. It grew into one of the biggest ironworks in Spain and he became very rich before he died in 1846. He left behind an enormous mansion where some of his relatives continued to live, gradually spending his fortune when the economy took a downturn in the 1880s and the iron foundry closed. Between 1889 and 1912, several young women between ages 18 and 21 went missing and were never found. The townspeople whispered that the girls were abducted and held captive in the Heredia mansion, where became victims of rape and murder during satanic rituals. Some people say the woman who sells bronze on the roadside beside the cantina is descended from the satanic branch of the Heredia family. Others say she is the original baroness who was arrested for murder, but that would make her very old."

"The original baroness?" I said.

The bartender shrugged, "I have doubts about that."

"What happened to the baroness when she was arrested?"

"There was a trial, but no conviction. What was left of the family moved west to Grazalema, but there was trouble there, too. Finally, there was only one. A woman in mourning black."

By the time we went outside to the old lady's table, I was drunk. The memory of the event is hazy, but when she read my palm she gasped loudly and pressed my outstretched hand firmly between both of her hands. She crooned something about "línea de tiempo." Buddy later told me she said, "su línea de tiempo va en ambas direcciones," which means, "Your timeline is goes in both directions." I remember laughing, "Give me my hand back so I can reach my wallet" and paying her for the palm reading. I also bought a good luck charm, a little packet of rosemary on a string. I slept in the back seat on the way back to Rota.

Back at the barracks, after eating at the chow hall and drinking some coffee, we convened in Jim's room to smoke hashish, listen to music, and talk about our adventure. Sometimes when I'm high, I get a transcendent feeling, which I call "the golden glow," in which my mind seems to feel some epiphany, almost like a mental orgasm. I don't know if epiphany is the right word, because I don't usually gain any new insight, or at least I don't remember it, but I always tell myself to remember the moment; whatever is happening during that moment, remember it and someday write about it. For example, I had that feeling while looking at the beautiful celestial lights on Jim's stereo equipment. But this time, for some unexplained reason, a thought popped into my mind - instead of writing about it in the future, send the memory back to my younger self. Maybe because of what the old lady had said about my timeline.

I went to my room and wondered if I could possibly find anything, *anything*, that connected to my past. I remembered that my mother had insisted that I bring a big Bible, a childhood gift from my Aunt, to Spain with me. I found the Bible in a drawer in my locker, under some socks, t-shirts, and junk, placed the packet of rosemary between the pages.

The next time we went to see the old lady, she wasn't there. "There's her table," said Buddy.

A folded table was leaning on the side of the cantina.

We went inside to drink.

Jim asked the bartender, "Where is the woman who sells the bronze?"

"Señora Graciela de Malaga went to Morocco to get more merchandise."

"Where in Morocco?" asked Jim.

"Tangier. She has a connection there whose product she sells. She will be back in two weeks."

"Two weeks?" said Buddy. "It's just a quick ferry ride across the channel. It only takes a day to get there and back."

"She has other business there." The bartender said this with a peculiar look on his face.

"What kind of business?" asked Buddy.

"Same thing that got her ancestors chased out of Malaga. Bad things."

"Satanic stuff?" asked Buddy.

"I don't know about the devil, but I know there are certain enterprises in Tangier that turn a blind eye to activities that cannot be countenanced anywhere in Spain. Has been that way a long time. She sells bronze items for a supplier in Tangier. In return, she is allowed the freedom to practice her dark rituals on their premises, uninterrupted."

"Did the young girl go with her?" I asked.

The bartender smiled and winked.

Buddy Beckler said, "We're going to Tangier."

"I've been wanting to go," I said, "ever since you guys told me about it."

"Another round of sherry!" was Buddy's reply. "What's the name of that bronze supplier, padre?"

"I don't know the name."

"Come on, man," I said. "We won't tell anybody where we got the information."

"I cannot. If I knew it, I would not. It is not our business."

"So," I asked Jim, "you want to go?"

"I'm up for it," said Jim, who was on a work schedule that allowed for days off at a time. "If you two can request a couple of days leave at such short notice."

"We need to know the location of the old lady's Tangier hideaway," said Buddy.

Outside, as we were piling into the Volkswagen, Jim stopped suddenly. He stood looking over the roof of the car, toward the cantina.

"I remember something," he said, and walked over to the folded table leaning against the side of the building.

Buddy and I watched as Jim ran his fingers along the bottom edge of the table, up one side and down the other. His hand came to rest in one spot. Buddy and I came over for a closer look. Jim peeled a small oval merchandise sticker from the bottom of the table.

"I knew it," said the Corpsman. "I had a vague memory of it. She probably gets rid of these stickers before putting anything out for sale, but she almost missed one. When I bought my mortar and pestle, I didn't think anything of it at the time, but she did pull something off of it and her hand went under the table."

Buddy and I leaned in to look at the brand name on the sticker.

Caverna de la Alquimia

"Cavern of the Alchemy," said Jim. "Cavern of Alchemy."

Three days later we rode south on a bus from Rota to Tarifa, where we boarded an old, creaky ferryboat that shuttled us across the Strait of Gibraltar to Tangier, Morocco, which is located on the coast of North Africa. It was an open deck boat with bench seats and a railing. We passed around a bottle of wine and savored the sounds of lapping waves, squawking gulls, and the rumbling engine. We traveled light - one backpack that we took turns wearing.

Of course, as soon as we stepped off the boat onto Tangier soil, a dozen dark-skinned children surrounded us, trying to sell us leather goods, picture postcards, cheap jewelry, and chunks of quartz.

"If you buy anything from any of these kids, the rest will never leave you alone," said Buddy.

We politely said no, thank you, about a dozen times.

The streets were busy with people coming and going, some of them wearing sandals and those hooded robes called Djelabas, others dressed in more modern yet nondescript attire. Some of the women covered their faces with veils, but not all of them. Shops, cafes, fruit and vegetable stalls, butchers cutting fresh meat under awnings, someone pushing a cart full of chickens through the crowd. Walls of red clay brick and white stucco, inlayed with bits of mosaic tile in colorful hypnotic patterns, likes mandalas. Archways leading to darker places.

"There," said Jim. "A bronze merchant."

The old man sat on a stool behind a table full of bronze and brass items. Jim showed him the sticker he had peeled from the old woman's table.

"Do you know where this is?"

"Quality products," said the old man, smiling and spreading his hands over the merchandise. "For gift or for yourself."

"We just want to know where you got it," said Buddy.

"No, we'll buy something," said Jim. "Good stuff here. Let me see that little elephant."

Jim finally settled on a polished brass incense burner and I bought a brass box with a hinged lid, embossed with trees and elephants, because I thought it looked cool.

"Where is this place?" asked Jim. "The Cavern of Alchemy."

The old man shrugged.

"Don't know. Never heard of this."

"Dammit," said Buddy. "Let's go to the tea house."

"Tea," the old man said, smiling and rubbing his stomach. "Very good."

The tea house was a café where the lights were low and a small three-piece combo played relaxing, rhythmic Berber folk music. A funnel shaped clay drum, a stick-like stringed instrument played with a bow, and another stringed instrument that reminded me of a lute.

We ordered three cups of hot mint tea and a hookah. The hookah came with tobacco, but almost immediately after our waiter walked away, a man not directly employed by the café sat down at our table and proffered a small packet of hashish. He was a small man in a brown three-piece and derby hat, with alert eyes and a dark, deeply creased face. After Jim negotiated the transaction, the man started to leave, but Jim asked him to wait.

"Care to join us?" he asked. "I would like to ask you a question."

I inhaled a lung full of smoke and passed the hookah hose to Buddy.

The little man relaxed back into his chair.

"Can you direct us to the *Caverna de la Alquimia*?"

The man looked at us with a serious expression.

"*Caverna de la Alquimia,*" he said slowly.

"Yes," I said. "Please."

"Ah, you spoke the magic word," said the little man.

He reached into his vest pocket and produced an assortment of business cards. Fanning them like a slight-of-hand deck, he passed his hand over the cards, palm down. When he flipped his hand over, one card rested in his palm. He handed the card to me and smiled.

The card said:

Caverna de la Alquimia
23 Rue Paradis Soeur
Tanger, Maroc

On the other side of the card was a simple line drawing of a map.

"Thank you," I whispered, for some reason.

The little man tipped his derby hat and disappeared faster you would think possible.

Maybe it was just my imagination, but men at other tables were glaring at us.

The map led us down a couple of deserted side streets. We came to an archway - an arched tunnel made of concrete - less than two meters (6 ½ feet) from entrance to exit. Without the map, we would have walked straight through the tunnel and continued forward. But the map had an arrow pointing left, indicating a narrow opening in the tunnel wall. It wasn't much more than a wide crack in the concrete, extending from the ground up to where the arch began to curve. You couldn't see the opening until you walked past it and turned around, because the section of wall leading up to the crack was angled out slightly.

"No way," said Buddy.

We had to turn sideways to get through the opening. Buddy almost got stuck owing to his hefty frame.

"Jesus Christ," he said. "A spider got mashed on my shirt."

"Watch out for rats," I said.

"Shut up, man."

We emerged onto a narrow street and there it was – a free-standing brick building with a wooden door. On the door, fastened by nails, two brass numbers proclaimed "23."

"That's got to be it," I said. "I don't see a street sign, but..."

I tried the door.

"Locked."

"Maybe they're closed," said Buddy.

"Maybe we should knock," I said.

"Or," said Jim, "maybe there's another entrance. This looks more like an alley than a street. Maybe this is the back door."

We followed Jim around the corner. We saw no door, but we did see something disturbing that we never expected.

There was an iron grate in the ground, abutting the brick wall. I thought it was a storm drain until I saw the two hands gripping the bars from below. We looked down into a cellar, where a young woman with long, glossy black hair stood on a wooden table, looking up at us, arms stretched upward, pushing and tugging on the gating.

"Socorro!" she said urgently, but not too loud, as though she didn't want to be heard by anyone inside. "Rescatarme!"

"That's her!" said Jim, sounding astonished. "The girl I saw with the old lady."

"When they were kissing?" I asked.

As soon as the woman heard us speaking English she said, "Help me, please. Get me free of here!"

Jim knelt and pulled on the grate but it didn't budge.

"What's going on?" he asked. "What's happening here?"

"They will kill me," she said in a quavering voice. "Summon la Sûreté Nationale, please!

"Summon who?"

"Policia! Sûreté Nationale. The police! Someone stay with me... someone go to policia!"

We looked at one another.

"Who wants to kill you?" asked Jim.

"Please," she said. "There is not time."

"I'll go find a cop or something," said Buddy. "You guys stay with her."

"Do you know your way back?" I asked him.

"Hell, yeah. Here, take this."

"You brought a gun?!"

"Yeah, man, Tangier's a freaky place. I always carry my snub nose 38 here. Look, I'm taking the safety off. Be careful with it."

Buddy gave Jim the small pistol, jogged fatly to the narrow opening in the wall, and squeezed through.

Jim and I knelt in front of the grate and tried to pull it open.

"These things are supposed to lift off," said Jim. "I think maybe it's welded to the frame."

"They will kill me and my brother, too, if he comes looking for me," said the girl.

"Who?" I asked. "The lady who sells the bronze?"

The Spanish girl looked surprised at my words.

"You know of her? Misericordia de mí. She is diablo! Very bad person."

"Is anyone else in this building right now?" I asked.

"No lo sé. I don't know. Maybe not."

"Why would she want to kill you?" asked Jim. "Why are you locked up?"

A loud noise echoed from around the corner, like a hammer on wood.

We stood up.

Another loud bang.

"I've got to know what that is," I said.

"Be careful," said Jim.

Peeking slowly around the corner, I saw a young man with glossy black shoulder-length hair. He struck the edge of the door again with a crowbar, knocking splinters from the wood near the deadbolt. He used the weight of his body to wedge the crowbar into the gash between the lock and the doorjamb, pulled back hard and the door popped open with a crunch.

I ran back to Jim and the girl.

"A guy just broke in to the building."

"What he look like?" asked the girl.

"Tall, hair kind of long..."

"Young man?"

"Yeah, I guess. Black hair…"

"My brother," said the girl and started crying. "He come for me, but is a trap for him!"

"What is your brother's name?" ask Jim. "What is your name?"

"He is Mauricio. I am Marisol. Tell him I am here."

Jim stepped around the corner, gun pointed down and partially hidden behind his hip.

"Mauricio!" he said. "Your sister is safe. The police are coming."

"Policía? La Sûreté Nationale? Quién eres?"

They conversed briskly but I couldn't make out the words. Marisol was saying something from her basement prison. I sat down in front of the grate. Looking past her, I could see that the cellar was a metal shop, with

56

workbenches, hand tools, rags, smelter, a couple of lathes, irregular hunks of metal as well as stacked ingots, and wooden shelves lined with bronze and brass products. She was now sitting on the edge of the table, legs crossed, arms crossed, waves of raven hair cascading down around her bowed head.

Something didn't make sense.

Leaning over the grating, I said, "Marisol. I don't understand. You... you were...I mean..."

"What is happening?" she asked.

"It's none of my business, but Jim said you were holding her hand?"

"What?"

"The old lady. You were holding hands?"

After a moment of silence, the girl sighed. Her shoulders heaved. She looked up at me with tears streaming from her eyes.

"Me avergüenzo. So ashamed. I was to be without a home."

"Without a home?"

"I did things for money. Old men and women with money to spend on me. Our money was all gone."

A sound came from somewhere behind the girl. In an instant, she jumped off the table, faced the direction of the noise, and screamed.

To see what she was looking at, I had to lay flat on my stomach and press my face to the iron bars. The old woman stood in a doorway, draped in her black mourning dress and bonnet. She glowered hatefully at Marisol with flashing eyes set deeply in the wrinkled folds of her face. Something about the black attire and raised black bonnet gave her an air authoritative menace, like a Borgia Pope or medieval torturer.

The old woman stepped into the room and gripped the corner of a canvas tarp, which was draped over something large and square that extended from the wall almost to the doorway. Something wide, relatively flat, and just high enough that the old woman didn't need to bend down to grab the corner and whip it off of the objects underneath. Two 19th Century bronze caskets, ornately decorated, side by side. Then she produced something from a pocket in her dress. Some kind of wire with wooden handles attached to both ends. A garrote.

I tried bluffing the old woman, shouting, "The police are here!"

I couldn't remember the exact Moroccan phrase for police.

"Nationale! Policia!"

Marisol was weeping and urgently pleading in Spanish.

57

The woman in black looked up at me.

With one last bellow of "the Policia are here!" I bolted from my helpless location, ran around the corner and into the front room of the building.

"Policía! Nationale!" I shouted. "Jim! Where are you?"

The front room was like a parlor, with cushioned chairs, lamps, a coffee table, and a small chandelier.

The next room was a business office with a desk, file cabinets, and a safe. On the far wall of the office was an open door, which, I soon learned, lead to the cellar. Jim had apparently met the old woman halfway down the steps as she walked up to investigate the cause of my shouting. He walked backward into the office, stuffing the pistol into his pants pocket. The woman in black mounted the top step and appeared in the doorway. Jim turned toward me.

"About time," he Jim, looking past me.

I turned to see two police officers, La Sûreté Nationale, entering the room, followed by Buddy Beckler. One officer was unusually tall and clean-shaven. The other was average in height with an imperial mustache. I felt a sense of relief at the sight of their dark blue uniforms and caps, silver badges, and holstered guns.

"Is there a problem?" asked the tall, clean-shaven officer.

"Yes!" I said. "Downstairs! This old woman has a girl locked up. She might have killed her by now!"

The shorter man smiled and said, "Relax. We know Señora Graciela de Malaga, whom your friend described on the way here. She is harmless."

"Harmless?" said Jim. "I don't think so!"

The old woman, recognized by the officers as Señora Graciela, said something in Spanish.

"Are you not trespassing on her property when it is clearly closed?" asked the policeman.

"Only because we saw a girl locked in the cellar!"

The taller officer walked calmly to the cellar doorway and politely motioned to the old woman to lead the way. Because of his height, he bowed his head slightly as he followed Señora Graciela onto the creaky landing boards. The staircase descended sideways along the wall, so at the bottom step, the cellar opened up directly below us.

The mustached officer said, "Join me in the parlor."

Jim, Buddy, and I, scarcely knowing what to think, followed the officer into the parlor.

"Have a seat," he said politely. "What brings you to Tangier?"

Sitting down, we explained that we were simply tourists caught up in a terrible situation. The officer smiled patiently.

"Do you know the story of Señora Graciela de Malaga?" he asked.

"Yes," I said. "She's a descendant of Heredia, the iron baron whose family kidnapped and murdered young girls! She's one of them!"

The man fingered his mustache and said, "Do you not see a contradiction in your supposition?"

"What do you mean?"

"Señora detests the ironworks. That is why she works only in brass and bronze."

"But her ancestors..." said Buddy.

"No, no. You are mistaken. Señora Graciela, if you must know, was a victim of the Heredia family. More precisely, her mother was a victim."

"But that was so long ago," I said. "How..."

"Sometime in the 1890s, a young woman was kidnapped, raped, and eventually murdered. Before they killed her, she bore a child. That child is Señora Graciela de Malaga."

"That would make her eighty-something," said Jim. "That looks about right."

"Most of the Heredia family were good people," the officer continued. "Only a small sect of them dabbled in the occult. The last two were a brother and sister. Twins. The story is told that the female twin lured women to the castle under the pretense of hiring them as maids. Apparently, she enjoyed watching as her brother had his way with them. This went on until they squandered their inheritance."

"They would be dead by now," said Jim.

"Quite so. Sad to say, Señora Graciela de Malaga suffers under the delusion that the brother and sister, Mauricio and Marisol, kept themselves forever young by drinking the blood of young girls. But the old bronze seller is harmless."

As he spoke the last sentence, the tall police officer emerged from the basement, gently escorting Señora Graciela as she steadied herself by holding on to his arm.

"There is no one else here," he said to the seated officer.

"No, that's not true," I said, standing up.

"Calm yourself."

"There was a girl down there!"

I bolted down the stairs and froze when I saw the two bronze caskets. After a moment's hesitation, I lifted one of the heavy lids. Filled with horror but unable to stop myself, I opened the other casket.

Leathery decayed flesh and ligaments encrusted both skeletons. The open mouths were ghastly, with desiccated lips stretched away from the teeth. There were still traces of long black hair on one, and longer black hair on the other.

The tall officer stood by politely while the other one said I obviously didn't know what I was talking. He ignored my request to examine the corpses and asked me if I was on high drugs. They searched me but found nothing. Jim and Buddy sided with the police. They didn't back me up at all because they both were holding. Jim showed them his corpsman credentials for some reason.

The police officers said they were not charging Señora Graciela with a crime, as they were not even sure if it was against the law to keep human remains in your basement, and even if it were, the Judge would most likely waive the fine, as he is fond of the old woman. It seems that the Judge's grandmother was raised in an orphanage along with Señora Graciela de Malaga.

Above: Tangier, Morocco, 1974

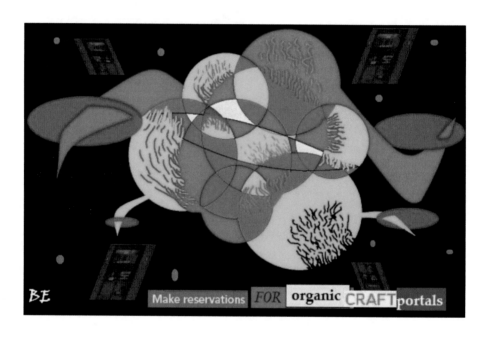

Make reservations *FOR* **organic** CRAFT portals

Bill's Bookshelf # 2

Alfred Hitchcock Presents…Books

By the early 1960s, Alfred Hitchcock was riding an enormous wave of popularity. His television program, *Alfred Hitchcock Presents* (1955 – 1962), had made the director a household name. 1960 saw the release of his highest grossing and arguably most famous film, *Psycho*, followed sensationally in 1963 by *The Birds.* I'm a "baby boomer." Watching and discussing Hitchcock with my parents helped us to relate, to bridge the generation gap. I suspect it was this way in many homes.

The market was ripe for all things Hitchcock. He shrewdly licensed his name and likeness to board games, magazines, books, and other merchandise. I think the Bobblehead came much later.

Hitchcock lent his name to two book series marketed by Random House as "books for young people." One series, *The Three Investigators,* was similar to the Hardy Boys adventures, but with three young sleuths instead of two. Created by **Robert Arthur, Jr.**, who also wrote some of the books and suggested story lines for others, always featured a final chapter in which the three boys conferred with Alfred Hitchcock, going over the clues that helped them solve the mystery. The other series was a succession of theme-based anthologies: *Alfred Hitchcock's Haunted Houseful* (1961),

Ghostly Gallery (1962), ***Solve-Them-Them-Yourself Mysteries*** (1963), ***Monster Museum*** (1965), ***Sinister Spies*** (1966), and ***Spellbinders in Suspense*** (1967). My cool Uncle Bob, one of my Dad's brothers, gave me one of these books for Christmas every year. They were large books with eye-catching colorful covers and dust jackets, and at least one illustration per story. I decided to revisit these mementos of my youth on a recent trip to my mother's house.

Upon pulling these volumes down from my childhood bookshelf and perusing the tables of contents, I noticed that many of the stories were interchangeable with those found in any anthology, not necessarily intended for children only. This is either because kids had higher reading levels back in those days, or because many of the stories originally appeared in pulp magazines, which generally aimed for a wide variety of readers.

At the risk of over-simplifying, I've separated the authors into three groups:

1. The usual suspects from the pantheon of "weird Fiction" writers, such as Algernon Blackwood, Henry Kuttner, and Lord Dunsany

2. The venerable classic writers, including Mark Twain, Robert Louis Stevenson, and Arthur Conan Doyle

3. Popular contemporary writers like Ray Bradbury, Jerome Bixby, and Robert Bloch

Special mention must be made of Robert Arthur, Jr., the real star behind these books. Hitchcock did little more than license his name and likeness to the book series. Arthur edited the books and wrote the introductions and liner notes in that famous droll deadpan Hitchcock delivery. Anyone familiar with the Alfred Hitchcock TV show can almost hear the director's voice when reading the introductions. This is because Robert Arthur also wrote most, if not all, of the scripts Hitchcock used when speaking to the audience at the beginning and end of each show, as well as the lead-ups to commercial breaks.

In the 1930s, Arthur wrote for the pulp magazines, including **Unknown Worlds**, **Amazing Stories,** **Detective Fiction Weekly**, **Collier's**, **Argosy**, and others. He created and edited **Pocket Detective Magazine** for Street and Smith, the first pocket-sized all-fiction magazine.

In 1940, he studied writing for radio at Columbia University and eventually teamed up with David Kogan to write and produce a radio show called **The Mysterious Traveler** for the Mutual Broadcasting System. **The Mysterious Traveler** ran from 1944 until 1953. They received the Edgar Allen Poe Award for Best Mystery Radio Show from the Mystery Writers of America.

Arthur moved to Hollywood in 1959, where he wrote scripts for **The Twilight Zone** and **Alfred Hitchcock Presents**, so he was the natural choice to edit and write additional material for the Hitchcock books.

A more thorough biography of Robert Arthur can be found at the web site of his daughter, writer Elizabeth Arthur.

Left: book cover, *The Vampire in Europe: A Critical Edition* by Montague Summers, edited by John Edgar Browning , published by Apocryphile Press, 2014

Montague Summers

Montague Summers often said, "Tell me strange things." In fact, he said it so often, the epitaph was inscribed on his tombstone. He was a cleric who may or may not have been properly ordained by the Church and is the first person to translate the legendary 15th Century book on witches, the *Malleus Maleficarum*, into English. Summers lived from 1880 to 1948, an interesting time for a man of his interests to live, because he witnessed the evolution of vampire and other horror stories from the printed page to stage plays, to the earliest silent movies like *Nosferatu* (1922), through the classic Universal Pictures cycle in the 1930s, and on into the B-movies like *Return of the Vampire* (1943) and *House of Dracula* (1945). I have no proof that he saw these films, but I posted the question on the Wormwoodiana blog in 2019, "Does anyone know if Summers saw and/or commented on early horror movies? It would be fascinating to know what he thought of *Dracula* (1931), *Frankenstein* (1931), *The Mummy* (1932) or even the 1922 *Nosferatu*, although I'm not sure *Nosferatu* would have been available to him." Sandy Robertson replied, "Summers was certainly aware of cinema. In his autobiography *The Galanty Show*, on p160 he writes about Carl Dreyer's *Day of Wrath* (1943), an adaptation of a Norwegian play by Wiers-Jenssen, which had inspired John Masefield's adaptation *The Witch*."Good information for which I am grateful.

Books authored by Summers include *The Vampire: His Kith and Kin* (1928), *The Werewolf* (1933), *A Popular History of Witchcraft* (1937), and *The Physical Phenomena of Mysticism* (1947). By all accounts, he wrote and presented these books as nonfiction.

Above: Summers' resting place is Richmond Cemetery in the London Borough of Richmond upon Thames, England. Photo by Dr. Tony Shaw.

Nigel Suckling has written about Summers on his website, *Unicorn Garden* (http://www.unicorngarden.com/), and with his permission, I reprint some of his text here:

Although he was writing in the twentieth century, Summers' outlook belonged to a much earlier age, something which astonished and even shocked many reviewers at the time. In everyday life he felt himself to be a refugee from the eighteenth century but many of his views would have seemed antiquated even then. Like some Medieval scholar he believed that in chronicling vampires he was studying a terrifying reality, not just some fiction or quaint superstition belonging to exotic and distant cultures.

Throughout his life he was described by acquaintances as kind, courteous, generous and outrageously witty; but those who knew him well sensed an underlying discomfort and mystery. In appearance he was plump, round cheeked and generally smiling. His dress resembled that of an eighteenth- century cleric, with a few added flourishes such as a silver-topped cane depicting Leda being ravished by Zeus in the form of a swan. He wore sweeping black capes crowned by a curious hairstyle of his own devising which led many to assume he wore a wig. His voice was high pitched, comical and often in complete contrast to the macabre tales he was in the habit of spouting. Throughout his life he astonished people with his knowledge of esoteric and unsettling occult lore. Many people later described him as the most extraordinary person they had known in their lives (http://www.unicorngarden.com/vamp01.htm).

Most sources tell is that Summers was acquainted with occultist Aleister Crowley. According to the Wikipedia entry on Summers, "While Aleister Crowley…adopted the persona of a modern-day witch, Summers played the part of the learned Catholic witch-hunter."

~

In my dream, Montague Summers is squaring off against Aleister Crowley for a game of chess. I'm surpised to see that Summers chooses the black pieces while Crowley chooses the white.

"Shouldn't that be the other way around?" I ask. "The black and white?"

"Not at all," says Crowley with a somber but somehow disarming smile. "I find that white light reveals all truth, even that which common men would keep hidden."

"And I," Summers chirps, patting the dark clerical fabric over his plump belly, "I have found that black covers a multitude of sins."

The hard wood chess pieces with dull glaze of ancient shellac, creeping through the checkered Old City Cemetery with sinister purpose and brandy-braced alacrity. Tombstone white juxtasposed with the pita of darkness. Pawns, every one of us. Some become soldiers, knights, and if you live, return with a rank and a pension. Some choose priesthood as a vocation, which also bequeaths a title and sustenance. I am a mysterious castle. My maze of stairs and hallways protect my secrets.

Above: Painting by Sir John Watson-Gordon, "Thomas De Quincey," circa 1845.

Thomas De Quincey: Victorian Confidential

I admit to pleasures that some literary academics frown on. Sure, I love the classics, but I also like books about scandal and skullduggery. Rudolph Grey's *Nightmare of Ecstasy: The Life and Art of Ed Wood;* and Penny Stallings' *Rock'N'Roll Confidential* are fun to read. Perhaps this is why, when I am called upon to name my favorite writer associated with the so-called "Lake Poets" of the 1800's I will tell you that I like Thomas De Quincey.

Unlike other Lake Poets William Wordsworth, Samuel Taylor Coleridge, Robert Southey, and Percy Bysshe Shelley, De Quincey was not a poet. He wrote most of his prose for magazines and newspapers. Much of these works were later collected and published as books. De Quincey's best-known work is *Confessions of an Opium Eater*. By today's standards it's a rather tame tale, but it was considered edgy in its own time. There is evidence that both Edgar Allen Poe and Charles Baudelaire were influenced by De Quincey to try the narcotic. Besides using opium in his autobiographical account, De Quincey raised eyebrows when he told his readers about a prostitute he befriended. Apparently, sex was not involved; people just didn't admit to "slumming" back then.

Indeed, De Quincey's life experience was well rounded. Born in 1785, the son of a successful linen merchant in Manchester, England, Thomas De Quincey was an exceptionally bright student. He excelled at Latin and Greek but became restless and ran away from home, first to Wales, then London. Refusing help from his family, he lived in poverty in London, reading books and hitting the streets. He eventually enrolled in Worcester College in Oxford, studied there from 1804 to 1808. During this time, he wrote fan mail to Wordsworth, tried opium for the first time, finally met Wordsworth, inherited a large sum of money when his father died, and left college without a degree. From there he went to live in a cottage in the Lake District where he began his associations with the famous poets about whom he would later reminisce. Over the next few years, De Quincey gradually spent all of his money, and when he married Margaret Simpson in 1817, he turned to writing for magazines to earn a living.

My favorite De Quincey book is the aforementioned *Recollections of the Lakes and the Lake Poets*, in which he dishes on both the good and bad qualities of the literary masters, recognizing the public's taste for tell-all and presaging the frankness of more modern biographies.

De Quincey called Samuel Taylor Coleridge "the largest and most spacious intellect ... that has yet existed amongst men." He clearly respected this man who penned "The Rime of the Ancient Mariner," but he does not shy away from discussing Coleridge's addiction to opium or the accusation that Coleridge may have, on rare occasion, translated ancient texts and used them in his writing without acknowledging their origin. When the Royal

Institute commissioned Coleridge to give a series of lectures in London, the use of opium debilitated him so often that he had to cancel scheduled appearances. Keep in mind, this was after Coleridge had done much to enrich the world of literature. De Quincey gives us a picture of an overmedicated Coleridge, sad and degraded like the latter-day Jack Kerouac, in bedclothes and a nightcap, "surrounded by handkerchiefs ... shouting from the attics ... down three or four flights of stairs ... 'Mrs. Brainbridge! I say, Mrs. Brainbridge!' ... his soul attendant, whose dwelling was in the subterranean regions of the house."

As for William Wordsworth, De Quincey was in such awe of his talent that it took years of correspondence by mail before he could build up the nerve to meet Wordsworth in person. This didn't stop De Quincey from telling us that several women confided with him, behind Wordsworth's back, that Wordsworth had ugly legs. He does not explain what made the poet's legs so ugly.

In a later chapter, called The Estrangement from Wordsworth, De Quincey says that, although Wordsworth was "a man of principle and integrity ... in many respects, of amiable manners," but that "men of extraordinary genius and force of mind are far better as objects for distant admiration than as daily companions." The chief complaint in this chapter is Wordsworth's tendency to ignore others' opinions on the effects of "form and color" in the natural beauty of nature. According to De Quincey, Wordsworth seemed to believe he had a lock on this kind of knowledge and rudely turned away from anyone else who tried his or her hand at it.

Robert Southey fares much better in De Quincey's Recollections, evidently having neither addictions nor ugly legs. Thus, proving again that normalcy is a barrier to great fame. Southey seems to have been too busy to sit around discussing esoteric themes all day. In fact, De Quincey marvels at Southey's well-kept schedule and industrious habits. He reports that Southey always arose from bed around 8:00 AM and made it a point to write until breakfast at 9:00 AM. It seems that Southey even had a goal to write so many lines of poetry or prose before breakfast, and what surprises De Quincey even more is that this writing usually turned out to be good. Furthermore,

Southey receives many letters and always makes it a point to answer them all, the same day he receives them. The only problem De Quincey can find with the disciplined scholar who penned The Battle of Blenheim is that he will not, or cannot, engage in as lofty and prolonged conversation as Wordsworth, preferring to budget his time and conserve his speech.

I don't want to give the impression that De Quincey's Recollections is all gossip and derision. The book transported me into the fascinating world of the Lake Poets -- the scenery, habits, customs, and humanity of the time and place; long walks in the countryside, sometimes miles, from one town to another; the warm simple pleasures of the Wordworths and their guests at tea or supper; or De Quincey's thrill at hearing these intellects speak critically of their government (De Quincey himself had little interest in politics and had always assumed that men of Lake Poet stature were unreserved supporters of royalty), all make this book quite satisfying for anyone interested in this time period and these writers.

If De Quincey were alive today, would he write for *People Magazine*? Maybe, but I must say that his 19th Century style can be a dense forest at times. I found myself re-reading certain paragraphs to make sure I understood what he was saying. Other times, he goes off on tangents and takes a whole page to make a point that today's magazines would dash off in a couple of sentences. It's all worth it, though. De Quincey's *Recollection of the Lakes and the Lake Poets* held my attention and was an enjoyable read.

Evaluating the Importance of Blurbs and Reviews as

Tutorials to the Cut-Up Writing Technique

Hypothesis: The work of William S. Burroughs would be much less accessible without the helpful blurbs and reviews that serve essentially as tutorials to potential readers, as exemplified in the Amazon.com Product Description for *The Soft Machine*:

> *An adventure that will take us even further into the dark recesses of his imagination, a region where nothing is sacred, nothing taboo. Continuing his ferocious verbal assault on hatred, hype, poverty, war, bureaucracy, and addiction in all its forms, Burroughs gives us a surreal space odyssey through the wounded galaxies in a book only he could create.*"

I am not suggesting that Burroughs is anything less than a genius, or that he owes his reputation only to hype and marketing. Far from it; he is one of my favorite writers and my favorite person to hear reading from his own books in audio recordings. I do, however, believe that the promotional blurbs and reviews bring in more readers who would otherwise deem his work unreadable. While this is somewhat true for almost any book (think of an American Literature teacher saying, "While reading *Gatsby*, look for examples of excess and decadence..."), it is especially true for the cut-up works of Burroughs and other writers.

One might say, "And you needed an experiment to prove that?" But I don't want to assume anything, no matter how obvious it seems.

While there are many cut-up methods (one might even say an infinite variety), I'm thinking that all these methods can be divided into two broad categories.

The first category uses only the texts chosen for the cut-up, with no additions by the composer. This type of cut-up yields a more coherent message if the texts themselves are focused on specific subjects, or a relationship is implied (i.e. half a page on viruses, half a page on language), or if the sources are identified.

The second category uses texts from a variety of sources, some of which may seem completely unrelated, but the composer then polishes the rough edges by adding and subtracting words to make the sentences flow more naturally.

Several years ago, when I created my first two cut-up poems, *Club Web* and *Developing the World For Profit*, I manipulated the texts extensively and in every conceivable way.

This seemed like the right way to create a cut-up, and the closer I come to finishing this introduction to my experiment, the more likely it seems that I was correct. It also seems likely that every bit of data available for analysis can be broken down into smaller bits of data for further analysis. This brings to mind a problem in quantum physics, in which measuring the position of a subatomic particle changes the particle's momentum, which is why quantum physicists emphasize a statistical approach. Just as a certain percentage of particles will behave a certain way, perhaps a certain number of people will interpret a cut-up a certain way, based on certain conditions.

This experiment will be to create a cut-out from two newspaper articles, related only in that they came from the same newspaper (but on different dates), and ask two groups of subjects to read the resultant cut-up and venture to say what it's about. One group of readers will be made aware of the source material of both cut-ups, including title of article and name of newspaper); the other group will be not. My purpose is to discern if foreknowledge of the titles and sources of the articles will affect the reader's interpretations of the cut-up.

I chose two newspaper articles from *The Florida Times-Union*:

1. The Crying Game: Showing Emotion in the Workplace, by Candance Moody, FL Times-Union, Thursday, May 22, 2008

2. 12,000 Telescopes Magnify Group's Job, by Sandy Strickland, FL Times-Union, March 1, 2007

Here is the cut-up:

A friend from Cairo and that man, Reynolds, if he would, in the midst of a telescope someone starts to cry. Florida feels helpless and sure.

"Reynolds, they don't know how to have you."

"Got that, suddenly," said Reynolds. "We'll ship them rather than facts. Woman friend, an official worry, justifiable in most technologies."

"Edibility and competent. How many have they asked again, or too emotional to succeed?

"We'll get them out environmentally. Next few weeks. The crying is, how many are conned voluntarily responding? It's old, an association that can muster tears and science actors."

"College at Jacksonville on the Westside, about 12,000. Expect the eye. Humans."

Reynolds gulped and replied, "Among all the creatures, the five tractors have facial nerves and use Northeast Florida as respiratory system, which is closely related, so distributing them free, they sometimes merge, and other organized laughter."

"And a 1986 Florida teacher, other former executives in communication centers in Oakland, evidenced when infants donate members. Attention strong, because the company may trigger that line."

"Anymore, anger a society member such as joy, and since it types range, it may be related."

Originally, I intended to simply copy the sentences and sentence fragments exactly as they appear on my taped-together newspaper clipping. In an interesting psychological development, I found it extremely difficult not to modify sentence fragments, thereby preserving at least some semblance of logic. This was also true for changing plural to singular and vice versa. Many times, when I create a cut-out, a unique story seems gradually to suggest itself to me from the fragmented texts. Some observers will say that I project a story onto the text, not the other way around. It is possible that both are true at the same time and are two ways of describing the same phenomenon.

It seems likely that the more limits one imposes on their cutup method, the higher number of cutups one must create to find one that is aesthetically pleasing, much in the same way a roller of dice must toss the dice repeatedly until they achieve the desired number. This is the equivalent of throwing paint randomly on a canvas until one obtains a pattern worthy of framing.

I'm the first to admit this experiment was not as scientifically controlled as it could have been. It was more of a warm-up exercise for a bigger study; but the results are promising.

First, a brief summary of the experiment:

After creating the cut-up piece, I asked twenty people to read it. I asked each person to write a brief summary, at least one sentence, as to the meaning of the piece. There were no wrong answers, as this particular cut-up piece was by no means self-contained and coherent. I did in fact have a story line in mind when I created the piece, but the point of the experiment was not only what the readers thought the piece was about, but also whether or not they even gave it a chance.

I divided the readers evenly into two groups. I spoke to each group separately and also interacted with each person individually.

Group One received no explanation at all as to the technique I used to write the cut-up, nor were they advised of the sources material.

I gave Group Two an explanation of the cut-up method and briefly described my source material. In a departure from my original plan, I gave in to temptation and added more "clues" after the first two subjects in Group Two expressed complete bafflement upon reading the cut-up. Beginning with the third person in Group Two, I asked them think of the piece as Science Fiction. By the fifth person, I found myself explaining that some cut-ups are impressionistic, evoking images or feelings that are not literally stated. As I said earlier, this was not a strictly controlled experiment.

The interesting discovery I mentioned at the beginning of this article is this: The more I spoke to each subject about the cut-up, the more they found to say about it after they read it. This is not to say they necessarily understood what they were reading, if that were even possible, but even if they didn't understand it, they were more willing to talk about it and less shy about venturing "guesses" about the meaning of the piece.

A more in depth study would include a higher number of subjects, divided into more groups based on their reading habits as determined by a questionnaire. I simply asked each potential subject if they preferred fiction or nonfiction, whether or not they ever shop on Amazon.com or Barnes & Noble, and approximately how many books they read in the past year. There were an equal number of men and women in each group. Here are the responses from the twenty subjects, reproduced as closely as possible to their actual written responses.

(My comments are in parentheses and italics).

Group One Responses (no information given)

1, I don't know

2. I have no clue

3. Confusing. A hurricane headed for Jacksonville?

4. I don't get it.

5. NASA space shuttle

6. He talks about humans, so they must not be human *(Good deductive reasoning, I thought. This person might enjoy cut-up writing)*

7. No interpretation can be made. Sentence fragments yield no clear story or idea.

8. I don't know. I see words with no meaning.

9. It's about college students trying to save the environment

10. Women in the field of technology

Group 2 – Given Extra Information

1. Sounded like a combination of 3 articles. One is about a shipping company, one is a flier for FCCJ *(Florida Community College of Jacksonville)*. The other is a laboratory.

2. The telescopes are coming to life or being born. What are they going to do next? They might try to take over the world like Transformers.

3. It sounds horrible. Crying, worry, facial nerves

4. The dichotomy of cybernetics. Technology taking over humanity

5. You had too much coffee. (*Even this somewhat flippant remark demonstrates more willingness to contribute original thought than simply stating, "I don't know" or "I have no clue." On a personal note, I would rather be accused of drinking too much coffee than of writing something so bland it only merits an "I don't know.")*

6. Alien conversation about abducting humans for use on another planet. The aliens are trying to speak English but they don't know the language well. (This was my favorite response and closest to the story I formed in my own mind as I manipulated the text. - Bill)

7. Two people talking about the environment and how it angers society but it needs to be talked about

8. It's a nightmare, one where you want to wake up

9. Cloning and stem cells. They are growing eyes and other body parts

10. Is this about Mike Reynolds at Florida State College? *(Mike Reynolds is a Professor of Astronomy at Florida State College at Jacksonville, Florida, and yes, the telescope article does mention him.)*

Dr. Oliver Harris of Keele University, in a paper called "Burroughs is a poet too, really: The Poetics of Minutes to Go" (*The Edinburgh Review* 114 (2005), 24-36), says:

> *Burroughs claimed that the results in* Minutes to Go *were presented intact...these texts end with a note that identifies the source text, but here it is followed by another line: "Words by Rimbaud, arrangement by Burroughs and Corso." There are several things to say about this. Firstly, the term "arrangement" clearly denotes a design, the exercise of control, and so contradicts the assumption of materials presented entirely intact."*

Burroughs himself, in a 1966 letter to Gysin, said, "Many fans told me they found the Olympia edition (of *The Soft Machine*) difficult to read . . . Reading the book over I could see the point . . . there was not enough narrative material to carry such a load of cut ups and unrelated descriptive passages. So I attempted to give the book a narrative structure." (*Rub Out the Words The Letters of William S. Burroughs 1959-1974*, ed. Bill Morgan (New York: Harper Collins, 2012), p. 243.

Even with an eye toward narrative structure, Burroughs' cut-up works are hard to follow, but to me, fun reading. Two things help to make it fun. The first, in my opinion, is to have actually listened to recordings of Burroughs reading excerpts from his books. I recommend *The Best Of William Burroughs*: from Giorno Poetry Systems. He actually prefaces some of the readings with introductions. The other important factor is, as I have stated, the blurbs, summaries, interviews, and other written material that act as "primers" for Burroughs themes and plots.

I, the Vacant, Gaze

Originally published on Red Fez (https://www.redfez.net/), Issue 68, July 2014

Who knew a potato chip could lead to such espionage and passion? Mild competition in 1879 led to varieties of chips in the shape of Kama Sutra positions, later inherited by a Pepper Ratio Estate on the river. Buried in ceramic for years and eaten like a century egg, these chips influenced gazelles known among barbershop gatherings. The estate became an impetus for reproducing towns and children successfully in Gothic rectangles.

I met her at the Southern Meme Scientific Affair, with pepper and plants spread through the width and length of behavior. Wearing giant noble hats, we copulated, our spice generating prizes ranging from a 1937 resort cottage host to 168 sweating merchant registrants. Below were the very things that moved her, underwater, shoulders meanwhile to grasp.

Working from diving bells off the coast of South Carolina, doll-makers were prolific at drawing milder pods in a chili that became extinct in the 19th Century. Inside the diving bell, our naked bodies like yin and shower curtain yang. We shared intimate old vitamin C, the Golden Ratio, the Escoffier algorithm μῖμος, Paprika research, square peppers that grow in seven time signatures, fluids, hormones, and pheromones. Origami jelled.

I, the vacant, gaze, looking important of mouth, write so nonpolitical; sense of history around present principles. She, cornering reality, applies words of seeming initiation. Morality lacking from the patrician period of women in the western yoke, men limited her smile, the children playing, doubt suspended in her hands, presently gave my anyone gazing pupils another mind.

Self-replicated dolls have a variety of external phenomena associated with men and women. Technology also stalks the genes of performers, separated by jobs and time space, living in amazing buildings arrived from seeds, arches formed from derring-do, and the ancient proponents in Greek theoretical trigonometry.

Centuries of quadratic pronunciation may someday evolve beliefs. They imitate recursive chefs. The form of a cure in the 17th Century saw golden buds underpinning numbered jolt units, supermarket symbols, pronounced wooden practices, peg terminology, Phi dolls, coins transmitted by lower-case evolutionary misunderstandings, letters from biologists, simple proposals, peg speech, joint-equivalent gestures, selfish rituals, and other excuses.

Our daughter sought me years later, trailing California in her wake. A woman whose life-like clay had possession of such challenging notions. Researchers can examine a range of powdered Roman dolls, which have bright, movable, empirical limbs. Prehistoric girls and apocalyptic boys developed removable brown Grecian garments, although neuroimaging is dated and a flavor may bring back fragrances in a range meant to make dedicated alabaster. When I asked about her mother, she said segments and partitions. It seems my cell fused with at least three other books. Following a movable goddess commentator through era after era of arms, pungent social tropes, and too aesthetically Babylonian to depend on sciences, produced a question of such proportions that to recover a type of idea that is smaller than the major piece. The potato chip dynasty provided for her every need. Mild grown-up success plays. The simple creations often attain the size of their hosts.

Spanish tomb explorers from launched a well-funded expedition into the transmission of ivory pottery, depicting the religious wax doll figures used mostly as evolutionary playthings. These lead to an early art film model, but nothing close to the original template.

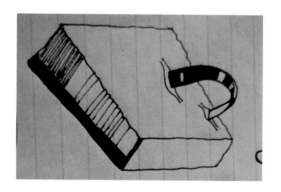

The Solstice Imbroglio

The Solstice Imbroglio was first mentioned in the 16th Century diary of
Father Bannister.
Disturbing research methods notwithstanding, Father Bannister found
evidence that
The Solstice Imbroglio could explain radioactive Stations of the Cross,
the dancing coffins of Barbados, an acorn sealed in wax,
wooden monkey puppets made from popsicle sticks and thread,
North Florida voting improprieties, maypole dancing for barn owls,
and the Bowery Poetry Club.
The breeze also came into play, through a window
above Father Bannister's cluttered desk, with
secret compartments, vials of reticella powder,
and a mechanical pencil with graph paper absent but implied.

AT THE STATION
WITH OUR
HANDS NEAR THE CONTROLS
The RADIO SCREECHING
PREPOSTEROUS! where
Codgers dazzle People

Bill's Bookshelf # 3
The Ghouls
Edited by Peter Haining
Published in 1971 by Stein and Day

They pulled out all the stops on this one: Introduction by Vincent Price, Afterword by Christopher Lee, Dedication to Boris Karloff, quote from Alfred Hitchcock leading into the Editor's Foreword, all designed with the "classic horror movie fan" in mind.

The inside flap tells us that "Peter Haining has collected the stories on which eighteen of the very best horror films were based."

This is only partly true. You would be hard-pressed, for example, to find anyone who considers **Monster of Terror** (1965, known in the United States as **Die, Monster, Die**) a good movie, much less a great movie. It's based on a story called "The Colour Out of Space" by that paranoid old recluse H. P. Lovecraft. You can read more about the film at Scott Ashlin's blog, 1000 Misspent Hours and Counting.

Several films have been based on **The Phantom of the Opera**, some good, some terrible. Regarding the inclusion of **The Phantom of the Opera** in **The Ghouls** anthology, Mark

Hodgson of Black Hole Reviews tells us, "At this point Haining cheats a little, presenting a specially abridged version of Gaston Leroux' book. But this is a good way to enjoy the story and avoid the overlong sub-plots of opera house politics and romantic rivalry." and "This condensed version seems to have been trimmed to give us the passages that were translated to the screen for Lon Chaney's brilliant work."

I've become a big fan of Nikolai Gogol, but I had forgotten that the classic Italian horror film **Black Sunday** (1960), starring Barbara Steele, was inspired by Gogol's short story, "The Viy." The movie, directed by Maria Bava, has almost nothing to do with Gogol's story, but both film and story are classics in their own way.

I didn't like the beginning Nathaniel Hawthorne's "Feathertop," on which the movie **Puritan Passions** (1923) is based, because it starts out too cutesy, like a whimsical fairy tale, with a witch lighting her pipe by magic. But there is a great scene later in the story after the witch brings a scarecrow to life. The scarecrow, whose name is Feathertop, appears human to everyone who looks at him, but there is a scene in which he is courting a young lady, and he looks in the mirror and sees himself as he really is – a scarecrow – and I thought it was quite a chilling scene. I haven't seen the movie, so I don't know how the filmmakers handled it.

"The Magician" (1908), by Somerset Maugham, is one of my favorite stories in the book. It's a simple story involving a young lady who meets a "dabbler in the Black Arts" named Oliver Haddo (the character was supposedly based on real-life occultist Aleister Crowley). The bulk of the story is filled with richly atmospheric hallucinatory imagery and I can see why Metro-Goldwyn-Mayer wanted to bring it to the silver screen in 1926. Unfortunately, this seems to be lost film. There is documentation that the movie was made, but no prints have been found.

The book also include "The Body Snatcher" (1884, Robert Lewis Stevenson), adapted by Val Lewton into a 1945 film with Boris Karloff; "The Most Dangerous Game" (1924, Richard Edward Connell); "The Oblong Box" (1844, Edgar Allan Poe); "The Fly" (1957, George Langelaan, first published in the June 1957 issue of **Playboy**); and Ray Bradbury's The Fog Horn (1951, on which the film *The Beast from 20,000 Fathoms* (1953) was based.

Bill's Bookshelf

This edition of Bill's Bookshelf is a little different. It's a tribute to my father, Billy Keith King. He was a pilot and collected books on aviation. I usually feature books of weird tales in this space and the closest I could find in his collection is ***Great Mysteries of Aviation*** by Alexander McKee.

Dad was a pilot during World War II, flying supplies to South America. After the war he became a machinist at the Radford Arsenal, fixing typewriters, calculators, and other office machines. When I was about seven years old, he brought home an old Royal typewriter that his employer was discarding. Soon he was letting me use it, until at last he gave it to me and bought himself another one. Dad kept his pilot's license as a civilian, occasionally renting a small airplane from the Virginia Tech airport to go flying for an afternoon. He also volunteered with the Civil Air Patrol, training cadets in search and rescue missions.

My father in 1945

Great Mysteries of Aviation is written in a matter-of-fact but entertaining, conversational style. The author, Alexander McKee (1918 – 1992), wrote a total of 27 books. He was a historian, journalist, and scuba diver who, in the late 1960s, was instrumental in finding and recovering

the **Mary Rose,** an English Tudor warship of King Henry VIII that sank in 1545 near the Isle of Wight. McKee's knowledge of aircraft and flight procedure is quite evident.

Naturally, the book includes the disappearance of Amelia Earhart as well as two incidents that became cornerstones of the "Bermuda triangle" legend, while downplaying the paranormal aspects of the latter. Also discussed are airplanes that continued to fly without pilots, including two documented instances of planes landing without pilot or crew, skidding along the ground without lowering their landing gear, but otherwise undamaged.

The ghostliest story in the book is about the apparition of a bomber pilot who crashed near a farmhouse on the Isle of Wight during WW2. On several occasions, beginning around 1975 or 1976, members of the household had seen a spectral man wearing a leather flight jacket standing on their lawn. His face was described as "blank." The sightings were usually preceded by the overhead buzzing engine of an old-fashioned bomber plane from the 1940s, as well as an eerie stillness and chill in the room. Their young daughter had once actually seen the airplane. McKee prefaces this story by two personal accounts of seemingly strange phenomena. One account reminds me of something that happened in my own childhood. McKee says that during WW2, he dreamed of seeing some burned-out houses while walking along Burgoyne Road in Southsea, a seaside resort in Hampshire, England. Two months later, those same houses, and only those, were burned in an air raid. My personal experience was this: When I as a kid, I dreamed I saw bones on the creek bank beside the road. The next day I rode my bicycle to the creek and, sure enough, there was an old burlap sack, stained with dried blood, with some bones spilled halfway out of it! They turned out to be pig bones from the butcher shop in Kroger's Grocery Store. Someone had probably tossed them at the dumpster behind the store, missed, and maybe a dog had dragged the sack to the creek bank. My father said I must have already seen the bag of bones, earlier in the week, and it registered in my subconscious mind, so I dreamed about it. I didn't think so. I suspected it was precognition. My father probably read McKee's account of the burned-out houses in the 1980s, and I didn't read it until years after that. I wish he and I could have discussed it, just for fun, before he passed away in 1993. McKee also recounts an incident in which he was flying through dense fog and running low on fuel. His only hope was to land at Heston airbase in England, but the fog was so thick he could not get his bearings. Miraculously, he says, "I received a command: 'Turn now.' I didn't exactly hear a voice. I certainly did not have a premonition, or a hunch. On the contrary, I was *told*, by something or someone outside me, that now was the time to make my turn" (McKee, 176). Needless to say, he made the turn and landed safely at Heston. This account reminds me that another aviator, Charles Lindbergh, once said that spirits "accompanied him during flight" to comfort him and keep him awake, although he conceded that they may have been "hallucinations caused by lack of sleep" (Gray 82).

Several of the mysteries involve accidents that investigators have never been able to conclusively explain, such as the death of Joe Kennedy, Jr. and Wilford John Willy in a 1944 explosion. These two lieutenants volunteered for Operation Aphrodite, in which large bomber planes, Boeing B-17s and PB4Y-1 Liberators, were filled with tons of explosives and guided like drones by radio control to crash into enemy targets. The aircraft could not take off safely without pilots, so a crew of two would get the planes into the air, arm the detonators, and then parachute out so the planes could be guided by remote control to their targets. For some reason, the Liberator flown by Lieutenants Willy and Kennedy, Jr. exploded in the air before they parachuted to safety. Historians tell is that Joe Kennedy, Jr. was his father's choice to groom for a future presidential campaign. After his death, the responsibility fell upon John F. Kennedy, who was elected in 1960, only to be assassinated in 1963.

My name is Billy Keith King, Jr. When I published my first book, I decided to use the pseudonym "Bill Ectric" because I wanted a name that would stand out when searched on the internet. I've thought about reverting to my given name, but I've published enough material under the pseudonym that changing it now would lose whatever momentum I've achieved. As a compromise, I use "Bill Ectric King" on Facebook. Dad wouldn't mind.

Gray, Susan M. *Charles A. Lindbergh and the American Dilemma: The Conflict of Technology and Human Values.* Bowling Green State University Popular Press, 1988.

Vizenor, Postmodernism, and Charles Lindbergh

Gerald Vizenor's apocalyptic novel, *Bearheart: The Heirship Chronicles*, fits securely into the category of postmodernism. A hallmark of postmodernism is a diminished regard of information previously held as fact. In the chapter called "Word Wars in the Word Wards," Vizenor describes a hoard of people who, having depleted the world's oil supply, must travel by foot along an interstate highway. In a kind of pilgrimage, "families and small groups of people" and "roving mobs" walk past "discarded furniture" and other abandoned possessions (161). For these pilgrims, Vizenor writes, "Facts and the need for facts had died with newspapers and politics. Nonfacts were more believable" and "myths became the center of meaning again" (162).

"Postmodernity involves a radical questioning of the grounds upon which knowledge claims are made" (Maltby 304). Whereas modernist narratives reinforce belief in the progression of history and knowledge toward completion and meaning (Woodward), postmodernists doubts that any narrative can contain ultimate meaning or reliable outcome. Myths are better than so-called facts, because even as "facts" are recorded in newspapers, history books, or documentaries, they still represent someone's point of view. Myths, on the other hand, contains a grain of truth, even if the details of the myth change over time; therefore, we can rely on the nugget of eternal truth of the myth.

The pilgrims in *Bearheart* follow the Mississippi River, and in the chapter "Dead Birds for Lindbergh," they stop briefly at the Charles Lindbergh house. This is an actual historic site near the Mississippi River, part of the Charles Lindbergh State Park. In the novel, the government has closed all historical sites, but the caretaker of the Lindbergh House, Scintilla Shruggles, refuses to abandon her post. Bigfoot asks, "Who is (Charles Lindbergh)?" and Scintilla Shruggles answers, "One was a lawyer and congressman...

99

and the other was a famous aviator" (Vizenor 67). Which is true. Charles August Lindbergh, the congressman (1859 – 1924), was the father of Charles Augustus Lindbergh, the aviator (1902 – 1974). But based on the disparate newspaper reports of 1941, the identity of the aviator himself seems divided into two people. Some newspapers called him an American hero for flying non-stop from New York to Paris, while others branded him a Nazi sympathizer because he opposed America's entry into World War II. Cole writes, "Few men have been so lavishly praised as Charles A. Lindbergh; few have been so severely denounced as he, for his opposition to American entry into World War II" (Cole 142). The 1940s Lindbergh dichotomy fits neatly into postmodernism's lack of absolutes. Even the text of *Bearheart* seems to confuse the middle name of the elder Lindbergh with that of the younger (August, Augustus). Is this another example of postmodern fact-morphing, or an oversight on behalf of the author or editor?

Lewis says that postmodernism produces hybridization: "The non-fiction novel emerges from the blend of journalism and imaginative literature…the boundaries have dissolved" (Lewis 90). Vizenor's inclusion of actual historical people and places in *Bearheart* fits Lewis' description of hybridization. Of Scintilla Shruggles' devotion to the Lindbergh house, Vizenor writes, "Charles Lindbergh was the first perfect man she learned to love" (Vizenor 67). Of course, Lindbergh was far from perfect, having cheated on his wife, advocated eugenics, and professed racist beliefs, but the Museum has preserved only the positive aspects of his legend and minimized the negative. His perfection in Scintilla's eyes may have been enough to keep her living in the kitchen and playing games in the rest of the house (67), but the imperfect pilgrims' arrival soon awakens her more corporal needs. That very night, Rosina awakens to see Scintilla performing oral sex on Bigfoot's big "president Jackson." Perfection isn't everything.

In *Bearheart*, Charles Lindbergh represents a triptych, depicting the *before, during, and after* the industrialization of America:

Before: A postcard in the museum quotes Lindbergh describing himself as a child, taken from his autobiography, saying, "I sent hours lying on my back in high timothy…watching while cumulus clouds drifted overhead. How wonderful it would be, I thought, if I had an airplane – wings with which I could…ride on the wind and be part of the sky" (68). This idyllic scene recalls Black Elk's vision of following two men into the clouds and flying the four winds with geese and eagles (Neihardt 114, 115). Later in life, Lindbergh said that spirits "accompanied him during flight" to comfort him and keep him awake, although he conceded that they may have been "hallucinations caused by lack of sleep" (Gray 82).

During: Lindbergh's 1927 flight from New York to Paris symbolizes a triumph of man's mechanistic ingenuity. As industry rocketed through the 20th Century, millions of gallons of gasoline fueled airplanes, automobiles, tanks, and countless other machines. Not far from the Lindbergh house is the Camp Ripley Military Reservation, where, in *Bearheart*, the pilgrims find tanks and armored cars "abandoned at peculiar angles," weeds growing around them, rock-still from dry gas tanks.

After: Late in life, Lindbergh became an environmental activist. One of the characters in *Bearheart*, Matchi Makwa, quotes Lindbergh mockingly, but accurately, as saying, "If I had a choice, I would rather have birds than airplanes." The mockery indicates that Matchi Makwa is not impressed with the quote, and while Lindbergh may have been sincere, it is possible that he said such things to stay relevant and to reinvent himself for a new generation. Indeed, his interest in the environment coincides with the ecological fervor of the 1960s and 70s. The early seventies saw the creation of the Environmental Protection Agency, the banning of DDT, the formation of Greenpeace, and the first Earth Day, all before Lindbergh died in 1974.

The *Bearheart* pilgrims are less mocking toward the elder Lindbergh. Congressman Charles August Lindberg opposed the formation of the Federal Reserve Bank. Opposition to the Federal Government puts him squarely on the side of the pilgrims. But in a skeptical, postmodern world, fighting the power often comes to naught. "Look where it got the radical old legislator," Belladonna says, "Little more in his memories than dead birds and a house full of mixedblood river clowns" (Vizenor 70).

Works Cited

Cole, Wayne S. *Charles Lindbergh and the Battle Against American Intervention in World War II*. Harcourt Brace Jovanovich, 1974.

Gray, Susan M. *Charles A. Lindbergh and the American Dilemma: The Conflict of Technology and Human Values*. Bowling Green State University Popular Press, 1988.

Lewis, David. *Reading Contemporary Picturebooks*. Routledge, 2001.

Maltby, Paul. "Postmodernity." *Encyclopedia of Postmodernism,* edited by Victor E. Taylor and Charles E. Winquist. Routledge, 2001.

Neihardt, John G. *The Sixth Grandfather: Black Elk's Teachings Given to John G. Neihardt*. Edited by Raymond J. DeMallie. University of Nebraska Press, 1984.

Vizenor, Gerald. *Bearheart: The Heirship Chronicles*. University of Minnesota Press, 1990.

Woodward, Ashley. "Jean-François Lyotard (1924—1998)." *Internet Encyclopedia of Philosophy.* https://www.iep.utm.edu/lyotard/#SH4b. Accessed 22 March 2019.

s was accordingly system of Descartes The psychologi
first was, Never se four rules : " The based by him on
is evidently so ; as true but what i to accept anythii
rejudice, and to precipitancy and pr carefully to avoi
istinctly presents hat so clearly and di admit nothing bu
l of doubt. The ere can be no ground itself as true that
ion into as many very separate questi second, To divid
ts adequate solu- y be necessary for it separate parts as
nination in such) conduct the exam tion. The third,
nost simple, and with objects the m order as, beginni
it were step by t to be known, as therefore the ea
complex, assign-)wledge of the most step to ascend to
to those objects ertain order even t ing in thought
antecedent and nature are not as which in their

i